THE MISSION

THE MISSION

A Film Journal

Daniel Berrigan, S.J.

1817

Harper & Row, Publishers, San Francisco

Cambridge, Hagerstown, New York, Philadelphia, Washington
London, Mexico City, São Paulo, Singapore, Sydney

Portions of this work originally appeared in Sojourners.

FIRST EDITION

Designed by Donald Hatch

Library of Congress Cataloging-in-Publication Data

Berrigan, Daniel.
  The Mission : a film journal.

  1. Indians of South America—Paraguay—Missions—
History. 2. Guarani Indians—Missions—History.
3. Jesuits—Missions—Paraguay—History. 4. Spain—
Colonies—South America. 5. Mission (Motion picture)
I. Title.
F2684.B56 1986   980'.01   86–45012
ISBN 0–06–250056–2

86 87 88 89 90 HC 10 9 8 7 6 5 4 3 2 1

To the Jesuits
for life

Contents

The Story of *The Mission*

The film was a modest enough effort, by the gargantuan standards of Europe or America. Required: two stars, eight supporting actors, and numerous extras, whether Indian or Colombian or Argentinian.

Then the director (a separate paragraph for him please!), a kind of living parenthesis, comprising beginning and end, including, excluding, minimizing, instructing, lending insight and outlook, orchestrating, being patient, demanding, outrageous—the right inevitable word, the right moment, the look that withers, the rewarding thank-you that makes of soul's best gift a privilege.

Then, plenitude—the earth and the splendor thereof. The limitless transport of decor. Across seas and through jungles and into the walled city come, like a magician's market on a lumbering elephantine cart, costumes by the hundreds; instruments of war, peace, and music; objets d'art; and antiques. The architects have preceded us by months; risen before our eyes, new creations crown the landscape in the city and in the jungle.

Then the necessary accoutrements of the European and American comfort quest; food, equipment for its preparation according to taste and whim, refrigeration, fuel. Then items and operators more nearly bearing on the task: technique, the thousand cables, transformers, filters, cameras, lenses, booms, generators; their trucks, drivers, and engineers; a crew of cameramen. And of course managers, assistants, and runners. Accounts kept, down to the last nut and bolt.

Every stripe and skill is brought to bear, like a burning lens, on the three or four minutes of any day, minutes that, like panned gold, will make one wild hurrah of the heart—the metaphysical point of it all, the heart of the world, the irreplaceable stunning image, whether done by face, gesture, or word. *Id propter quod omnia.* When it happens, we are gods.

The Jesuit state of Paraguay was signalized by a fervent spiritual life. Economically, as early as the eighteenth century, it was an industrialized state organized on the cooperative principle. If it had survived, Latin America would have advanced nearly a century. From the social and political viewpoint, it provided a model of unquestionable democracy; and what is more, a democracy of indigenous people (Lacombe, *Science Ecclésiastique*, 1955).

At the opening of the film, the Jesuits had been in South America for some hundred and fifty years. A map of the continent will show the vigor and range of outreach: from the Guarani tribes north of Buenos Aires, to the Casanari, south of Bogotá, along the spine of the Andes and the Spanish frontier. The map would also show the Jesuit influence in the vast parallel territory of the Portuguese. There too, but with growing fear and unease as the slave trade was legalized, they pursued the work of evangelizing, adapting, experimenting, building, writing their treatises and dictionaries and diaries and letters, and extending a welcome to the surrounding tribes.

Every so-called spiritual undertaking is hemmed in by a veritable thicket of worldly perplexities, especially if, as in the missions of the Jesuits, a strong cultural and political connection, an interplay of interests, joins priests and chancelleries.

The church–state agreement may seem at first glance a rather simple matter of mutual advantage and aid. The dangers grow as these seemingly compatible interests, the prospering of the two kingdoms, appear in their true light; invariably they are not mutual (or mutually exclusive) in practice. Nothing so neat, to say the least. The "incarnation of the church in the world," the world as attentive hearkener to the gospel, always on the point of conversion—this benign theory of the "two powers" is by no means the final word of the gospel on the nature of each. Nor can it be asserted that the history of the church vis-à-vis the state bears out the theory in practice. Quite bloodily to the contrary.

Nor, to push matters further, could one easily demonstrate that the church is at its best and holiest when the kingdom of God and the kingdom of this world walk tranquilly through time, hand in hand. In such instances, an unpleasant word occurs with regard to the celestial partner: betrayal.

Talk about the two peaceable kingdoms! We have come a long way on the Christian road since that Friday ironically named Good. On that day, toward the middle of the first Christian century, Rabbi Jesus was made the tormented object of capital punishment at the hands of the state. Thus were Christian origins illumined by such a death endured at the behest of the "benign kingdom."

Talk also about distances, spiritual light-years! The Jesuit missions, the theme of the film, are one interesting measure of the distance traveled on that meandering road of history, the inextricable network of byways, detours, shortcuts, the tunnels and fords, the interweaving of assumptions, theories, theologies, the military, political, and social dead ends. Did the roads lead toward two kingdoms, or one? Why not indeed, make one kingdom of the two, marry heaven and earth, and end the vexing schizophrenia once for all? For long, worldly, altogether brilliant interludes (including the Jesuit missions), the marriage seemed indeed to have been consummated.

Then, as the film sets out to tell, the extraordinary experiment of the missions came to a catastrophic end. For a century or more, the mission flourished; it shed light on the civilized world, acted as reproof, exemplar, and ideal for Europe and America. Then something awesome occurred, almost a freak in nature. A kind of immense continental plate began to shift and groan underfoot. One continent or two? It had been one. It was shortly to become two. The Kingdom of Spiritual Grandeur, so to speak, was utterly destroyed by the Kingdom of Legitimate Force run amok.

Thus our film. And thus the lesson, which may still be of moment. The geography of the Two Kingdoms, all and any confabulations of ecclesiastical and civil Merlins to the contrary, does not place them peaceably side by side. This is no accurate map of the Jesuit missions, nor of any equivalent arrangement known to history. Such a map is named Nevernever. The map may look persuasive, but one must be wary, keep a third eye open to something known as the real world. There, alas, one cannot but note the blurring of frontiers; the Two Kingdoms overlap, collide, challenge, encroach.

So the tensions grow, unperceived, unattended to, in proportion as prosperity lulls the two parties, their sycophants, generals, cardinals, and theologians deeper into an ominous dream.

Either of two outcomes may be thought to follow. One is the sorrowful, but strangely cleansing "peripeteia" of which the film tells. The armies move on the mission and destroy it; the Jesuits are seized, jailed, shipped back to Europe in chains. Many of them die in prison. Mutuality, reverence, all the clichés, catchwords, and concealments of church–state politesse stop here. The church has dared be itself, a community of succor and resistance and sanctuary for the powerless Indians. And the state, in consequence, was obliged as well to show its face: a warrior's. Thus was the truth made evident, another Friday named Good.

A different outcome was possible. One can be grateful that the Jesuits, for all their tragedy, were spared this. Its cynical form is enunciated by Dostoyevski's inquisitor, that persuasive clone, part imperial church, part imperial state. He speaks for the terrible Other Outcome: in effect, a kind of liturgy, the public burning by the powers of one kingdom (the other complicit) of the gospel itself.

On the Paraguayan missions, the Jesuits served at the pleasure of the crowns of Spain and Portugal. The "pleasure" was of course official cant; other, less favoring moods betimes clouded the royal brows. Meantime, the rhetoric became a kind of rubrical stereotype, on both sides strikingly similar. Virtuous intent was both invoked and praised; "their Christian majesties" were congratulated ad nauseam for guaranteeing not only the welfare and safety of the missioners, but also the freedom of the Indians. Thus went the pavane, a rhythm of charm, and, for well over a century, it was of considerable substance.

But there was a debit side to all this. Inevitably the debt gathered interest, to the point of usury.

The debt accrued around such indefinables as whim and

mood, a whisper in the royal ear concerning "red gold" (Indian slaves), rumors of Jesuit silver mines, of illegal coinage and taxation on the mission. The whispers were a strange mix of real envy and feigned horror—violations of sovereignty perpetrated with impunity by the impudent. Thus the debt accumulated and there would inevitably arrive a day of reckoning.

Indeed Jesuit labors and achievements on the missions were so widely bruited about, romanticized, enlarged upon as to create in Europe, almost by spontaneous generation, an opponent and opposite number, an Iago to their Othello. In Portugal the great whisperer was named Pombal; in Spain, the count of Aranda; in France, de Choiseul. It was a strange success that bred, like armed warriors sprung from earth, such figures of ruin.

The theme of the film is thus set in place: the destruction of the mission. In this awesome task, many elements came together: European courtiers and kings, expansionist, assured beyond doubt of the benefits accruing to the "savages" through such worthies as invaders, conquistadores, gold rushers, mercenaries, and freebooters (these were always accompanied and in due measure mitigated by the preaching of the faith of our fathers); then too, European settlers battening on the slave trade and slave labor; "mamelucos" (surely the rootless, violent "contras" of their day)—all these found common cause and sealed the outcome.

Toward the end of the eighteenth century, a new treaty arrangement was devised in Europe. Among its provisions was a shift of colonial Spanish-Portuguese borders. For ratification, the pope's approval was vital. The pope's delegate, Altimirano, duly arrived in Asunción and summoned all parties to a public hearing. Question: should the new treaty be ratified, or not. The Jesuit missioners, sensing the gathering storm, traveled in numbers from distant areas.

According to the film, the tone of the exchange was at times heated, and even on the part of the colonials brutal. In spite of the best efforts of the missioners, the question of questions was severally ignored or derided—the welfare of the Indians.

When the issue of Guarani survival is raised, as it is repeatedly and with moving eloquence by the Jesuits, such intervention is received with contemptuous laughter.

Possession is nine points of lawlessness. The Europeans are in possession—of vast land holdings, of gold and silver, of that human commodity they call "red gold," Indian chattels to work the haciendas and mines, illegally in most cases, beyond doubt immorally.

In Spanish territory, slavery is illegal; but Spain is providentially distant and accounting is hard come by. In consequence, in both colonies, illegal or not, slavery is, by a further irony and outrage, beyond reach of the law.

The law comes up for cursory mention in the Asunción episode. Then the settlers get down to cases, the real subject being, under a thousand synonyms and subterfuges, power. The presumption is clear: the colonists may dispose of their "possessions," buy, sell, barter, transport, misuse, separate spouses and children one from another, work them to death, as self-interest and ego dictate.

Power—the question hovering in the stifling air of the courtyard. How to best succeed in carving out ever larger pieces of the continent, populating one's acres with the profitable labor of slaves. In so elevated a quest, the Portuguese and Spanish find common cause, lay aside their enmities.

A less pleasant matter—who dares stand in the way, impeding these sensible worldly developments, comprising as they do the "advance of civilization"? The Jesuits must be destroyed. As for the Indians—they are something less than human in any case. Open season will soon be declared.

Meantime, there is the new treaty, with its fresh border arrangement. The treaty is of consummate interest both to Spain and Portugal; it signifies the healing of old wounds and rancors; it will make brothers of born thieves. And above all, it will remove the Jesuits once and for all.

The treaty of 1750 trapped the Guarani Mission in a kind of no-person-land. They had no legal existence on their present lands, nowhere to go. A vast and prosperous experiment, the first and possibly the last of its kind, was suddenly declared expendable and cast like chaff to the winds.

A momentous decision faces the papal delegate, Altimirano. Are the missions, reasonably safe and undeniably flourishing under the Spanish crown, to be transferred to the Portuguese as boundaries are shifted? The second option is hardly more attractive: the ousting of Indians and Jesuits from their homelands and the attendant achievements of nearly two centuries.

Father Gabriel argues passionately against either of these nonchoices. If Indians and missioners remain in place, the missions fall into the net where slavery is sanctioned. And if they consent to the exodus, a grim prospect lies ahead: the abandoning of seven towns some thirty thousand Indians put on the road—exile on a monstrous scale.

This is the text of Clause 18 of the treaty:

From the villages which his Catholic Majesty cedes . . . the missionaries will leave with all their moveable property, taking with them the Indians, to settle in Spanish territories. The said Indians may also take their moveable property and the arms, powder, and ammunition which they possess. In this way the villages, with their church, houses, buildings, and property and the ownership of the land, shall be given to the Portuguese.

Both missioners and Indians hear the crack of doom. They have explored the land offered them by the Spanish; it bears no comparison with the riches they are asked to hand over under the draconian ruling. They are to abandon a veritable garden and undertake a perilous exodus into an uninhabitable wasteland.

The adversaries of the Jesuits, Cabeza the Spaniard and Hontar the Portuguese, press their case relentlessly. The treaty must prevail, the missioners must be made to obey. And when might His Eminence, Altimirano, (wily Hontar poses the question) be expected to announce his decision?

Altimirano, a man by no means for sale in this sordid flea market of special interests, is not to be hustled along. His decision: he will delay a decision. He will first see for himself this fabled mission. He will accompany the Fathers on their journey homeward.

The vast social aspects of the destruction of the mission come to focus, as in every film worth viewing, on the lives and passions and triumphs of a few individuals. In *The Mission*, public agony bears down on the fortunes of two Europeans.

The first is a certain Mendoza (Robert De Niro), quondam slave trader and murderer, who has stormily converted and is now seeking entrance into the Jesuit Order. The other, the saintly Father Gabriel (Jeremy Irons), is superior of a remote Guarani mission. After his conversion in Asunción, Mendoza abruptly abandons his past and casts his future with the missioners. He joins them in their return from Asunción to the mission, undertaking the punishing trek through jungle, mountains, and rapids—but with a difference. The celebrated convert chooses the guise of penitential fool; he fashions a symbol of his detested former life and drags it along—a sack bulging with his armor and weaponry.

Father Gabriel views the bizarre spectacle with tranquility, but the other Jesuits are appalled. When they make their objections known to Gabriel, he sternly invokes his authority: Mendoza is free to follow the Spirit in whatever unpredictable mode he needs to do so.

Thus by boat, portage, and mountain trek, accompanied by their Indian guides, the missioners proceed home. A vagrant hope buoys them: Altimirano, though diplomatically withdrawn, seems far from hostile. In a mood somewhere between dread and hope, the little band arrive in the Chaco to a joyful welcome from their neophytes.

A splendid homecoming indeed: song and dance, a tour of the workshops, the mission church, the flourishing orchard, and fields beyond. Altimirano professes himself moved beyond words.

But Altimirano has read the writing on the church wall, traced by implacable hands in Asunción. The mission is doomed. He must salvage what he can, mitigating a disaster fast approaching.

He issues his order: the missisoners are to return with him forthwith to Asunción. They are further commanded to announce his decision to the Indians. They must also exert their considerable influence to prevent armed resistance and urge submission to the regime of the Portuguese.

The announcement is pure desolation.

Some Jesuits obey, as do a number of the Guarani. Others resolve angrily to resist.

A pivotal scene between Mendoza the novice and Father Gabriel whets the issue. Sparks of anger fly. Mendoza reverts to his old self; he must stand with the Indians, come what may. Gabriel, a resolute blade, yields not an inch. He accuses Mendoza of renouncing his vows and declares in effect that "either nonviolent love is at the heart of the Christian message, or there is no message to offer."

There follows a parting of the ways, the severing of friendship; the blade has reached both hearts.

A furious battle breaks out on land and in the rapids. Mendoza, armed to the teeth, his back to a wall of flame, dies.

Gabriel, surrounded by his people, prays in the mission church. Finally, he takes up the sacrament, the symbol and presence of his unarmed God. He and the Indians proceed in solemn rank to face the massed renegades and mercenaries.

In front of the torched church, Gabriel falls like Mendoza —and so unlike—each within sight of the other.

Two deaths, an unanswered question—unanswered in their century and ours. In my estimate (a not altogether neutral one, to be sure) it is to the honor of the film and its makers, that the story purposes to settle nothing. Its task is more rigorous and

more modest—to raise questions, to summon the intelligence
and evoke the moral capacity of its viewers.

Any instruction on the omnipresence of bloodshed, for
those who live in this bloodshot century, seems to me strictly
redundant. Countless innocents have died before their time, in
hideous ways. We the living must be accountable for the cost
as best we might, live with it, do what we can to limit the
rampage.

Thus reflection joins us to the eighteenth-century mission of
Gabriel and Mendoza; it's a a universal setting, a haunting déjà
vu. The mission, it seems to me, is an accurate image of Nicaragua and Afghanistan and Northern Ireland and South Africa.
Also of England and America. Armies mass from the four
winds, determined to "settle matters." The absolute justice of
this or that cause is invoked—invariably by both sides. War
ensues, but the matter to be settled remains as it was, a crisis
inviting another sanguinary round.

"Just wars," in our century, waged with the weapons we
have ghoulishly stockpiled? A noble friend recently deceased,
Carroll Dozier, called the shot on the illusion: "The 'just war'
theory must be filed away in the drawer that conceals the flat
earth theory and the theory of the sun traveling around earth."

Inded the nuclear armageddonists are hideously closer to
the bone of our predicament, closer than those who justify an
arithmetic of allowable murder. So is the mad motto: "One
more war, once for all."

Nor can it be claimed that Christians or Jesuits or actors or
filmmakers or any of us humans have at our disposal today, any
more than in former times, a superior wisdom that might tip

the scales in favor of human survival. Alas, church and state, citizens and believers, skeptics and unbelievers, we have blood on our hands as a matter of history, and nukes in our hands as a matter of polity.

In us Gabriel and Mendoza live on and register their passionate and contrary choices, as well as the consequences thereof, choices that mysteriously form, deform, and reform us, that continue to determine both the outer limits of historical understanding and the soul's moral style, determine moreover who is to play icon and who iconoclast, and why.

The film, whatever its public fortune, seemed to me an honorable venture, a rare, even unique undertaking. It dares to raise questions both crucial and neglected: how humans choose to live, and for whom, and with what resources; also how they choose to die, and for what vain or dearly purchased cause—the pivot, the vexed, tormented, central question of all.

INTRODUCTION

It was an interlude rare enough. I was dwelling in my urban aerie one day, savoring a few hours of quiet. And just then the phone rang. In my experience, this clamor often sends a signal; one rhythm is ended; another is about to get underway, and abruptly, at that.

So things went. The caller was Roland Joffé, director of *The Killing Fields*. Would I be available for a discussion on a film proposal? I would.

The project was a script by Robert Bolt *(A Man for All Seasons, Doctor Zhivago, Lawrence of Arabia)*. The story line concerned the European Jesuits of the eighteenth century, and their fabled "Jesuit Republic." And might I be interested in taking part in such a film?

Robert De Niro was to play the lead, Mendoza, a difficult part indeed: murderer, dealer in "red gold" (Indian slaves) turned wild-eyed Christian convert, turned even further to an aspirant in the Jesuit Order.

And eventually De Niro's counterpart was found. Jeremy Irons would portray the redoubtable, wise, clear-souled Father Gabriel, a counter to the darkness, chaos, and death-ridden despair of Mendoza.

A proffer was made. Would I travel to South America for the period of filming, some four months? Would I act as advisor to the director and actors on matters relative to the Jesuits?

A long story, a large commitment. A sense both of burden and possibility. So I went.

*   *   *

"The Jesuit Republic." "The Jesuit Utopia." "A high degree of civilization." "Everything held in common." "They knew nothing of gold or silver." "An extraordinary perfection." "A paradise." The achievement has been put in many ways by both friend and foe of the Jesuit Order.

The facts at least are not in dispute. In 1550, a brief decade after the foundation of the Order, the Jesuits arrived in Salvador de Bahia. Thirty-five years later, they were working among the Guarani, a vast confluence of various tribes. Throughout South America, these tribes were eventually to become a living network of Christian converts, and were the chief "parallel developers" of the missions.

Much ink has been spent in defending or attacking the passionate "missionary urge" of the Jesuits. Undoubtedly, arriving in the New World as they did under the more or less active protection of the crown, the Jesuits were subject to numerous ambiguities, chiefly, that of the cross following on the flag. Undoubtedly they were also sons of their time, enthusiastic royalists. The arrangement, as far as can be judged, was never in question, nor was its complex consequence, for weal and woe.

The weal developed slowly, but irresistibly. No capital punishment in the *reducciónes,* as the new, protected settlements came to be known. Also no currency, no private property. In sum, no mere aping of European societal arrangements.

And could it be that the denial of pride of place to possessions, egoism, and lethal sanctions was the mysterious source of every good thing that followed?

In any case, the good things astonish. Churches were built that rivaled the splendor of European cathedrals; streets were paved; the miserable hand-to-mouth existence of the Indians yielded to a settled rhythm of harvest and planting. Add to these the singers and musicians and builders of instruments who delighted sophisticated European visitors. Also add flourishing trade, and communications by road and river far exceeding anything in existence in the same areas today . . .

Closer to the burden of the film, much ado arose concerning the role and character of Mendoza. Would the Jesuits, jealous of the honor of "Ours," have admitted to their ranks a confessed murderer and slave trader? Even granted a spectacular conversion, the fiction of the film demands a large suspension of fact.

In the course of our filmmaking, very dromedaries of contention were lashed through these the needle's eye of dubieties.

Such matters are of course not easily settled, perhaps never finally to everyone's satisfaction. Much depends on the range and rhythms of attraction, holiness, fraternal devotion, and largeness of spirit which the film is able to summon.

Nor can it be ignored that the conduct and character of pre-Christian Mendoza bears a startling resemblance to that of another figure normally thought of in rather more cloudy terms. Mendoza reminds one of a certain Spanish hidalgo of a slightly earlier period. This prototype, whose rake's progress included at the least sexual adventurism and military bloodletting, is known to history as Ignatius Loyola. He went on to found the Jesuits. And to be acclaimed in the church as saint and mystic.

All of which would incline one to reflect that in the realm of grace the facts sometimes surpass the wildest fictions. Further, that in such matters it behooves canonists of what can and cannot be to tread warily.

Baldly put, our film attempted a straight-faced impossibility: a two-hour summary of a hundred-and-fifty-year achievement. Absurd. And at the same time sublime in its assumption that the camera can almost instantaneously create such images as will capture and convey vast portions of time and space. Further, that the actors can be brought to a pitch of comprehension and be lit so vividly that moments, hints, phrases, mere parts will convey the resonant whole.

Maybe. And then again maybe not. The fiction, in order to come true, must exist also in the eye of the beholder. And when the nearly instant images play surrogate for the ever so slow trudge of the human, we have good reason for skepticism. Can it be that the ascent toward God, understood as a lifelong, difficult trek, has become, through the Miracle of the Wondrous Eye, both cheap and available, your friendly neighborhood commodity in fact? Is a film a species of wonder drug?

Maybe a glimpse is only a glimpse after all, and not to be confused with such weighty matters as the human trek, the exodus from enslavement toward grace and glory. Maybe, in other words, we can be modest even about the achievement of our immodest technology.

When things go as badly as they do today, it becomes a diversion for many, including makers of films, to transform political and moral powerlessness into phantasmagoric images of power, savvy, and control. Indeed the soul must have its food; and when the soul is rendered inglorious and degraded, it feeds on that garbage whose trade name is dreams of glory.

In contrast to such weird extravagance, a film, if it be truthful, can offer only a gleam, a hint. And a hope.

The eighteenth-century Jesuits made in a wilderness a haven for a decimated and defeated people. A haven and more. The missions were also a splendid, embodied image of soul. Which is to say, the Jesuits created for all to see, to praise, condemn, or emulate—an image of the majestic humanism and generous variety of their own spirit. A universe without corresponding to a world within.

And as the world judges, it all came to naught. But, this granted, a point of interest remains. The same world that renders such judgments, also brings the judgment down, a blow of churlish demigods. Fire and sword, covetousness and control, hatred of that "other" whose moral superiority is an affront; these are the crosswinds that bring utopias "to naught." The winds blow, noble enterprises fall, a tragic circle is closed. And finally, prophecy is in shards. Horrid *anangke* has won.

We latter-day Jesuits, lesser sons of giants, are grateful for a mere gleam of greatness. We know our scope, how miniscule it is. We know the humiliating contrast that exists between ourselves and our noble forebears. We Americans have been brought low by America.

If we cannot emulate, the times being slavish and ourselves hardly free, we can at least celebrate. And out of celebration, even of our defeats, we can take hope.

The film teaches the harsh lesson, better still, implies it. And not merely or even primarily to the Jesuits. Modesty, thoughtfulness, and a sense of limits, whether in the director, actors, producer, camera, or viewer, are symbols of something great and elusive, something the times place indefinitely beyond us, a gleam, a hope, a grail in midair. Follow, follow. Our humanity is assaulted, cheapened, sold for pottage across a thousand counters. But it is still in our power to cry out and reclaim.

Thus the film. Modest despite an almost suffocating splendor. Modest in that it eschews all pretension of answers, formulations, solutions and concentrates at its best on the dark interplay of hearts, a terrain no mortal can walk without wariness and dread.

No easy solutions, no cheap grace. Mendoza and Father Gabriel die, violently. The meekness of one is no protection, anymore than is the fierce arrogance of the other. We have here in the decision of the filmmakers, in their unwillingness to play God, to create heroes or antiheroes, to stroke the one and damn the other, a rare and laudable wisdom. They have been true, as the saying is, to the way life goes. Especially today.

But if the deaths of Mendoza and Gabriel run parallel, their lives do not; and herein lies a capital point. Gabriel dies. So did Martin Luther King and Gandhi and Stephen Biko and Archbishop Romero and uncounted thousands of others of our lifetime, for whom retribution, even so-called self-defense, is equally anathema.

And others die like Mendoza. He stands with all who take up the sword as a matter of principle, of despair, of communism or anticommunism, of faith gone wrong, of chivalry, of plain worldly logic. His name is legion. It is ideology and power politics and "just war" theory and deterrence and window of vulnerability . . .

The film, then, refuses to take sides. No one stands condemned or vindicated; the angel of death hovers over criminal and virtuous alike.

The theme, all told, is simplicity itself. It attempts to illumine one way of life, or perhaps two ways. Out of each will issue, as flower from root, a manner of dying. In the matter of death there are no exemptions, only differences. The differences are of moment, the film dares hint. And that is very nearly all.

Such modesty offers large benefits of integrity and good

sense (and, one is tempted to add, good theology). Indeed, modesty survives our most unlikely history, survives somehow. It may yet, despite our monstrous folly, redeem an immodesty that to our ancestors constituted the primal sin, the mad revolt against one's proper place in the scheme of things. Pride, and then the fall.

We are not yet, in spite of all technological pretension, capable of inhabiting the earth peaceably. Let alone indeed able to make of that world the modest utopia that humans at their best and worst never quite give up on.

Utopia? Jesuit republic? Kingdom of God? We have been brought low; we would settle for less today, for something even slightly superior to political authority off the rails, nuclear weapons underfoot and overhead; the means polluted, the end deranged.

Shall the human prevail against such odds? History offers a certain austere hope. Such a "republic," a "utopia," a vision perilously near the "kingdom of God"—once, rarely, or a few times, for tragically brief interludes, the noble images and impulses were verified in our world.

The images are never quite defeated, which is a way of saying men and women refuse to give up. In the "basic communities," in the Catholic Worker, in the Plowshares movement, in the Sojourners communities, as well as in that trackless world of pain and disappearance, of hope deferred and heroism unquenched—in these the "reducciónes" of the Jesuits live. In honor and dishonor, in life and death.

Thus the film celebrates memory, the present, the prisoners of conscience, the martyrs, all who renounce pernicious well-being and the middle way. To all such, we send a blessing. From them, we receive one. And with them, we go on.

APOLOGIA

Came an offer, cutting a four-month slice
out of my whole-grain life.
Would I voyage to the Colombian jungle, the Argentine waters,
to advise and consent (to differ, raise mild hell)
in uneasy consonance,
to assemble a scattered myth
the bare bones of the heroic dead?

Who could tell if spirit escaped
split skulls, rent bodies, tempest and travail
to haunt our history, advise, consent, raise holy hell
in the misspent, misshapen world,
edgy, sputtering, intent on dealing
the knockout blow

to the Mount of Blessing
and the Man of the Mountain,
to the Maker and Walker of waves
to the pearl of price
the plenteous harvest
the groaning table
of the Kingdom banquet.

Therefore came.
Would have the pearl
agleam in the mind
and the prodigal boy
in tears reconciled
and the wretch by the road
unaccountably succored.

and Jesus the weaver
of chansons de geste
undisplaced by dissonant
artisans of ruin.

Jesus striking
like a blind harper
the song of the end
who sees in the dark
of days, the light.

The heroic dead.
A vagrant hint, a gleam of spirit,
a playful beckoning; why not come?

Therefore came.
    Steep, steep the way.
   Pursue the gleam. The story half told
  retold. And over and over
and again and again.
And no way out.
And "I am the way."

The Journal: The Making of *The Mission*

I arrived in Cartagena, Colombia, on Easter Sunday evening, to be met at the airport by a bustling crowd of movers and shakers. In the midst of everything chaotic and torrid, it was a joy to see the wide smile of Roland Joffé riding above it all like a transmogrified Cheshire cat. Such a good start could only augur well.

My own assignment seemed reasonably vague, given the fact that I was landing on an unknown planet, as an unknown species. I was to be available for the actors who were to play Jesuits in the film, helping them dissolve to a degree the enigma and folklore surrounding the Order. I was also to play a Jesuit myself, in the minor mode.

The former task was not long in getting started. Roland suggested that Jeremy Irons and I spend some time in solitude; luckily there was a massive Jesuit history in Cartagena centered about the church of San Pedro Claver. We repaired there, were shortly made welcome, and settled in for thirty-six hours of silence and reflection. We centered things around the famous *Spiritual Exercises* of Saint Ignatius, which every Jesuit reads and undergoes with considerable thoroughness at the start of his training.

I found Jeremy a ready spirit, very supple of mind, a listening being who went away silent and returned curious. We discussed among other matters sin, redemption, guilt, responsibility. We dwelt a long time on the meaning of faith, which appeared to me as a kind of unexpected intervention, a third party, so to speak, entering an impasse and bringing, if not relief, at least a measure of light and hope.

We returned to what many are pleased to call real life, in this case, the work being pursued in the courtyard of another splendid colonial church, Santo Domingo.

There a throng milled about, a meld of many nations and tongues and skills of every conceivable kind. There were nuns in dark bustles and brimmed hats. The workers were busy about a multitude of tasks, from connecting a veritable spaghetti knot of wiring to scrubbing the courtyard floor.

I'm told I'm welcome to use one of five directors' chairs, occupied as I am in observing the goings on, taking notes on wind and weather and voice and conduct and outcome, readying myself to cast a vote on this or that scene.

Last night one of the actors, a mettlesome spirit from New York, offered the corps of actors a six-course "bash" to celebrate the start of our work. I decided that despite the world (or perhaps because of it) I would get in step with the others, though I must confess that the supply of the heart's helium is at a new low. I celebrate with the others, yes, but strictly for my own reasons, thinking as I do constantly of our dear ones in prison, those dying in the hospice at St. Vincent's in New York, the homeless women at Holy Name Shelter. My landmarks, my seamarks, my very sanity.

Someone asked shortly before my departure for Colombia, "Can you in good faith leave those who so need you just to make a film?"

I said as simply as I knew how, "Yes, I can. They're in better hands than mine." I wandered about the courtyard, in wonderment at the complex clotting of skills and machines transported across continents and seas, all to be assembled here in a colonial cloister that hasn't reverberated to such commotion since slave days, to be sure.

HOW THE MISSION CAME TO BE

Someone raked in a veritable World Bank of pesos, and
    brought the impossible to pass—
    The crossing of continents and their intervening seas
      was done in a flash.

Costumes from Italy, hundreds of wigs descending on sensible
    and daffy heads.
    And the food! shrimp in the jungle and ice-cream cones for
      children and the childish and their dads.

Class distinctions honored like ten commandments at
    a punctilious port royal—
    Actors dined with actors, workers sat on their hands,
      Colombians perched like parrots on the lowest rung of all.

A fiesta! spectacles and astonishing stunts by
    night and day,
    The Indians swam the air like fireflies, the altitudinous stars
      said their silvery say.

And the pesos fell, a tropical rain, a Holy Spirited British
    Protestant sign—
    predestination or some such, under the camera's omnivorous
      eye.

Then the canisters rolled like wheels of Ezekiel, heavy with
    auguries across the seas
    Rolled up jungle and ocean and bird calls and tarantulas,
      in short, all of us.

Life was a lark in Eden (except for spiders and serpents,
    except for the rumor, the wrong jump, the odd pratfall)—

> Time catapaulted, world syncopated; a ripe mango in a
> shaken orchard. Immortality is all!

There are trunks filled with trinkets and artifacts, splendid gowns whizzing by on equally splendid bodies, peasants, seminarians, grand ladies, and functionaries (the latter surely the ancestors of yuppies, primitive briefcases, noses in air, an atmosphere of impenetrable wisdom). The workers pull and push things about, in a very frenzy of "getting things right."

A crew of vandals, one might think at first. But there are signs posted about the town signed by the filmmakers, Gold Crest Studios, apologizing for inconveniences to the citizenry and promising to restore all properties to their original order.

Ancient saddlebags and equine gear, plastic hosing, old leather-bound volumes, cameras, lights mercilessly glaring down, a host of suns. A madonna and child gaze from a portal fantail, bemused, apart, finished images of the human, no doubt in wonderment as to this fever of the instant.

In any case, a question arises: are we dumb as the fabled dormouse running backward in time, finding the present beyond sense or sequence? Or is it true, as a friend said to me, that the cinema can deal adequately and fairly only with the past, the present being "too much with us"? . . .

Muskets and musical instruments, tools of every heft and use. A cleaning woman wanders through shaking her head in incomprehension at this outer-space landing on her terrain.

Someone snatches up a gigantic raw carrot from a paper sack and proceeds on his way, munching as he goes. It all looks like chaos, as I suppose a hill of ants does at first glance. But if one has patience, hangs around, order emerges, things come together.

Roland choreographs, allowing everything its proper scope. A word here, a gesture there. It works.

Indeed, they know what good work means, these British, just as they know how to celebrate. A new style of empire, after the collapse of the old. At the same time, it's salutary to reflect that the American film folk expend equal resources largely on junk. Here there seems to be access to artistry and substance.

Jeremy last night, "You'll be there for the filming tomorrow, won't you? . . . And you'll tell me if the slightest bit of ego mars things." I'd reminded him of such triumphs of non-ego as Schofield in *A Man for All Seasons* and the stars of the French films *Diary of a Country Priest* and *Monsieur Vincent,* of the seemly and luminous modesty of those roles. He listened with great attentiveness. I think his face has greatly changed during these days; gone is every trace of the stagy and edgy. Now a peace, earned and acceded to, dwells in him.

The cameras started rolling about 9:15 next morning. A scene between Jeremy, the Jesuit, and Cheri, the lady seeking help, her lover having been murdered by his notorious brother, Mendoza. The two, the grave and measured priest and the lady at a loss, stood in the cloister doorway in concentrated stillness. Many takes: each to the uninitiated, at least, looks very good.

Jeremy approaches me afterward, "How did it seem to you?"

"I thought the last one wrapped it up."

"So did I."

The police lean perilously over the arches, along with everyone else, to catch a glimpse of the actors in the cloister below. Salvation? The image as savior?

* * *

The perishing heat. The sun a floating furnace. And the great smoking orbs beating down from their stilts. A subaltern (never the director) barks, "Stillness! No need of moving about! Still!"

The spectators lean forward perilously from their height, like a frieze of humans. One of the kliegs begins to hum and sputter. "Cut it!" Roland huddles with the actors; they stand stock still in their finery in the shade. Beautiful inward faces, caught in the splendor of a moment they create, inhabit, slowly let go.

Moni, the Cambodian actor, and I talk at length about his part, a Guarani Jesuit who, in the film, is named superior of the Europeans. He asks how such an appointment would have been received. It seems to me that it would be understood as a moment of glory, when the university of the church and the Order would be vindicated; assimilation without contempt or racism. Henceforth, an Indian will hold authority over the others, something far different from being received in their midst as an equal. In fact, this appointment would be seen as a first step leading to the withdrawal of the missioners in favor of an Indian province of the Order.

The camera on its high dolly is like a wheeled centaur, all-seeing, fiercely recording the jots and tittles of mortals, judging, grimacing, in charge of things, so to speak.

From what I can see, Jeremy is doing well; the residue of ego is going up in smoke.

I watch and ponder, and a few questions occur:

·Does the dictum "more is less" not apply here? Which is to ask, could an extraordinary film such as *The Killing Fields* have been made with more modest means to even greater effect?

·Can an assault on the senses be construed as favoring contemplation?

·Indeed, has any film in history made us (makers or viewers) more apt for spiritual or social change? (Perhaps the question is off base. Films after all, according to one peculiar theory, are modes of entertainment, not instruction.)

·Are films today only another example of the triumph of widening technique? Are they an example of questionable means over ethical ends? I have a half-articulated sense that the culture wants death "popularized" in all its idioms, varieties, incursions, gratifications . . . Does such florid meticulosity only serve, as conspicuous consumption invariably does, to destroy all spontaneity?

·*The Battle of Algiers* must surely rank as one of the noblest examinations on record of the conquest of the oppressor by the moral superiority of the oppressed. Yet when I last saw the film in my neighborhood, the Columbia University students in the theater raised a gross cheer every time a bomb went off in restaurant or market. And when the film was ended, these ersatz warriors in Plato's cave returned beyond doubt to their stereos and pot sessions.

Two athletic workmen climb the top of the garden wall, there to hold branches in hand and cast wavering shadows on the faces of the principals. They squat there motionless, like benign gargoyles, which requires a considerable discipline, since the surface is not flat, but sharply peaked.

It's a cause of wide grins and more that I prefer to go about barefooted; it can't be credited that a Jesuit so disports himself amid the formal splendors of the old city. Ha!

*　　*　　*

Roland's slight figure in the midst of more or less contained chaos, a leaf in a storm. He is smiling, no matter what; he gives a generous tone to everything.

An edifying reflection is in order. In 1965 I was shipped off to these shores by order of Cardinal Spellman, my delict being a rather visible opposition to the Vietnam War. The intemperate speed with which I was disposed of quite reduced me for a time to a kind of human detritus—dust, ashes, and desolation. Evidently my absence was to make war easier to wage with the concurrence of the church. My absence, so to speak, would make many hearts fonder—fonder even of me, as long as I was absent.

I find it impossible to describe, even to myself, the atmosphere of those sulphurous hours, hours like weeks, weeks like years. The heavens remained closed, turned to adamant; no rain fell.

It was a time of death on rampage, not only in Vietnam. Death followed close, the death of friends. An entire family of friends perished in Mexico by asphyxiation shortly after I had visited them. Then months later, as I approached Bogotá to meet with Camilo Torres, he was murdered.

My present circumstance is, as they say, something else again. I come here as a teller of tales to the necromancers. They seek someone who knows the secret, a potion out of the Jesuit pharmacopoeia to work its magic on the actors. It goes without saying that they, being deprived children of our generation, have never downed so magical and renewing a brew, brought up as they've been on lukewarm dregs.

No wonder Jeremy's face turns inward, like a flower at sundown. He's had his day, so to speak; but the night will instruct him in the sleep of the gods, their dream of a beloved creation.

We passed a day in the so-called Courtyard of the Inquisition. A great to-do on foot and horseback, as De Niro and Aiden warm up their pacers. A bronze tablet on the wall of the place informs that these were the headquarters for some hundred years of a peculiar Spanish institution. Under its hammers many died, many more lived in terror, and a number of unfortunates were converted to something known as orthodoxy.

They do the scenes piecemeal. If a prop or a setting is useful, time itself is shifted about like a piece of scenery, and we are months into the past or the future. Sequence—moral, physical, or temporal—counts for little. What is counted as important is absolute, meticulous historical fidelity—such and such a room or backdrop or costume. There is a great jolting of time in favor of place. In this scene, for example, a minor hero perished before he had fairly drawn a breath—at least in the film.

This dislocation places a double burden on the actors. They must not only step into another century; they must also snatch at fragments of imagined time, and then let go. Something like puppets whose masters have flung down the strings.

Jeremy and I passed another quiet two hours. We discussed discipleship (the word is too long for comfort); we talked about trust and belief and giving oneself to a community. Then, "Who are the Jesuits and what is it like to be one?" he asks.

I ventured a few confidences, heart in throat. In my worst hours, it appeared to me that the Jesuits were created by a kind of necessity in nature, a spontaneous generation occurring in Western culture itself. And this not merely to confer a blessing on the eruptive ego of Europe. Jesuits would be the "light-armed cavalry of the church," in the regrettable metaphor.

To be sure, being a muscular arm of the post-Reformation church, their outreach was to be primarily "spiritual," a word on which they were shortly to confer a new and startling definition. The definition, as a matter of history, would be at times worldly, practical, and visionary.

We would even produce from time to time a spectacular rogue Jesuit. To the relief of the Order, he would usually be shown up as entirely out of whack, since the vast majority of Jesuits at any given time were apt to be devoted workhorses, living and dying in harness to their Bible and their *Exercises*, in sum, to the glory of God.

These, the vast majority, and not the paltry few who betrayed, were the puzzle and the triumph. Any Jesuit worth his salt would regard them, his brothers, as beyond all praise, his feeling for them too deep for words. It was these unknown and unsung laborers in the vineyard whom our film properly set out to celebrate; it was toward their springs of life the actors were to find their laborious way.

The others, a few in every generation, were another matter, a matter perhaps not worth lingering over. They were great self-seekers; given the main chance, they seized on it and in effect betrayed their brothers. It frequently pleased these spectaculars, after their departure, to write books in which the Order was portrayed as a darksome enigma. The authors of such revelations thereby became briefly famous.

I noted on the wall of the Palace of the Inquisition, engraved, together with the cross and palm symbols, a curious apologia. I translate rustily. "Terror and incarcerations and loss of property and even an occasional 'auto-da-fé' are admitted. But these, and worse, are excused or dismissed [as the account goes] by defenders of the faith [among whom, one suspects, is the composer of this revelation]. The Inquisition is in fact [again, the sense] no more inhuman than other institutions in vogue in Europe at the time."

Thus went the elegant rhetoric of complicity, immortalized on the courtyard wall. The room just off the yard bore a sign above the door: "Place of Torture." I entered, half expecting a display of instruments of infamy. Nothing of the sort. All the gore and glory were removed. But I went cold nonetheless; so blood-ridden a history is not easily exorcised.

I was walking in the old city, when from a balcony the Jesuit pastor of San Pedro Claver church shouted my name. "Come up, come up!" A smiling family, including numerous children and a grandparent, welcomed me. We settled in our box seats to witness the spectacular shot: Mendoza and his cohorts dragging and running the captured Indian slaves into the marketplace of Asunción.

Alas, there is shortly heard the unnerving basso profundo of the assistant director, "MISTER BERRIGAN, OUT OF SIGHT PLEASE!" Whereupon everyone laughs, and we flee inside.

The slave traders thunder down the narrow street, a great commotion, a rake's progress. Mendoza is upright in the saddle, arrogant as Satan on parade.

It terrifies me—it is too close to the original. The headlong contempt, the sense of an early evidence, a hint of how we got where we are—horses rearing and plunging, slaves subdued in despair, the sword. And that ship of fools named "our history" is launched.

That the Indians should mime their own enslavement? What are their thoughts, as they are dragged along in the dust, singly or bound together through the Cartagena street, on foot, hand bound to hand like a generational chain of destiny, or roped hand and foot, naked, riding backward on horses?

A procession of anguish and guilt; not a fiction so much as a fact. A fiction that with meticulous industry is aimed at reproducing a fact.

But the fact is so portentous as to lead to a mystery: the infection of time and this world by a sin called "original." It is the poor of the world, of Colombian favellas, who are on horrid display here. The Indian extras, noble as they are, and pitiable in their dignity, are existential stand-ins. Fact, fiction, symbol—all three. And at its deepest, as the missioners understood, is the outraged dignity of Christ himself, in his least children.

Interminably, generation upon generation, the chain gang of humanity passes by; the original sin is rendered ingeniously original once more; there are new ways of death, new bonds forged, new slaves made captive.

A cold comfort of sorts comes over me; the slave traders, in their malign zeal, are miming their own enslavement. The scene is shot over and over, the bellow heard time after time, "Action! Clear the street! Cut!"

Do the Indians think of the bitter past, how and when this all got underway? If they do, it seems to me more pitiable still, comparing their lot today with the part their ancestors were forced not to play, but to live and die under.

And a question must arise in their minds: "Are we not today, some two hundred years after, still being shunted about by the economic slave traders?"

The following occurred to me as a valid analogy. A woman, the descendant of prostitutes and herself a prostitute, is hired by foreign filmmakers to play a prostitute. The film in question was written about her and imported to her country. It is of little consolation to her that she plays her part brilliantly. She knows this. In the eyes of the satraps of illusion, she has become a necessity; but as a human being, she is no more than an indispensable afterthought.

They think of her, that is to say, only as long as necessity lasts. This is what it means to be an afterthought—even while one is being thought about.

A long, serious discussion last night at supper with Susan, the British casting director, on the role of Gabriel. He chooses at the end of the film not to take up arms in defense of the threatened Indians. But in so choosing, he must avoid giving the impression of a weakling, that in fact, he has no contravening tactic to offer. And if the film so ended, with no effective alternative offered, it would be little more than a glorification of violence, its romantic apogee.

So went her argument, which I found somewhat unconvincing, never having considered nonviolence a matter primarily of tactic, let alone of successful tactic. The supposition in this case seems to be that unless Gabriel can come up with a successful outcome, on the spur of the moment, his moral choice is discredited. But who says so? Certainly none of the classical agents of nonviolence, from Christ to Dr. King. Still, their resistance against injustice and their eventual acceptance of death at the hands of the violent has apparently failed to take hold as an acceptable tactic—especially, it must be noted, among Christians.

More breadth, less depth?
Still, the widest screen in the world, be it wide as the world,

can tell us little or nothing about the meaning of the world.

One thinks, by way of contrast, of so modest a thing as a good book and its available hieroglyphics.

She is earnest and intelligent, and she blazes across the table like a rising planet of truth. She had undergone all manner of religious disciplines; for six months she had trained with Sufi dervishes.

"And why did you leave off?"

"I got lazy. But they were offering nothing of interest in the way of studies—even studies of their mystics or scriptures."

"And since then?"

She'd gotten intrigued by a group of Cambodian Buddhists, and all but bewitched by a famous English Dominican. "He had a face like a smashed tomato. And when I went to the loo, I found beside the toilet the works of Karl Marx and Freud."

And later, "They're all alike after all, aren't they? I mean religions . . ."

I was quite sure they were not. More, that her wondrous, so modern shortcuts were a shortchanging—not only of the religious history of the race, but of God, and finally of the laws that govern a human life, her own, laws that are to be taken, if at all seriously, then step by step.

Without becoming portentous, there is a true God and there are false gods. And all betrayals of the true God by God's purported people do not negate the existence of the truthful One.

She was a seeker. She shone on high, amid the shadows and images that seem, especially here, to be our peculiar lot and burden.

*   *   *

Now here's an entrepreneur of some note! He's a property owner along the street in the old city where the entrance of slaves and traders is being filmed. This gent refuses to move when the word booms over the horn, "CLEAR THE STREET!" And worse. By no means quelled, he actually issues forth at the precise moment when "ACTION!" sounds, for all the world like a final trump. He strides up and down the street as fancy takes him, toward or away from the camera (it makes no difference as to his direction; the take is spoiled).

Indignation explodes around him. No matter. Possession, including self-possession, is nine points of the law. With marmoreal calm, he states his case: a million pesos as the price of his absence. Now let us concede that the presence of a superstar is worth many millions of pesos, but the absence of an otherwise unknown? Of a double negative, the shadow of a shadow? The crisis is apt to tie the cerebella of economists and logicians in knots.

Thursday, April 18. Viewing the remains of St. Peter Claver in the church named for him, one feels how fatally easy it is to dismiss him a second time from this world. Such wretched art, so harsh a revenge on goodness! According to the images, he was treacly and morally boneless, a do-gooder armed with food, drink, and Band-Aids, all aimed to produce a slavish flock of Christians. The latter (again in accord with the art) were admonished to have "patience with their lot," assured that their chains and fetters nicely dovetailed with God's will. According to this Supreme Slavemaster who hovers over the paintings like a celestial Simon Legree, the slaves are to advance toward their torment in the mines and plantations singing the praises of their estate and its Fabricator.

Nothing of course could be imagined further from the truth of Peter Claver—and of his God. Pedro was, if not a troublemaker, at least an interloper in the domain of greed and gelt. He was a passionate political being; his life is a clue—perhaps the indispensable clue—to the great and tragic developments of a later century. These must include the understanding among the Jesuit missioners that they could protect the Indians only through segregation from slave traders and the white race generally. Then there was the growth of furious opposition against the Jesuits, in consequence of their success in the protected towns.

I see Claver as seminal to the Jesuit enterprise. His political understanding was evangelical, humane in the highest degree, practical and visionary at once. He put his body where his words were. He followed through, undertaking immense treks across country, to discover the well- or ill-being of the slaves he had met, fed, succored, healed, instructed, and defended on their first landing in Cartagena.

He refused to allow baptism to become a kind of front behind which greed could throttle the helpless. In consequence, the slave traders came to hate him with a vengeance. But since he had the forethought to appeal to the king of Spain on behalf of the slaves, his work prospered, at least for a while.

Peter Claver,

I come to your catafalque, out of encompassing darkness,
a desert place.
Our need is your virtue, the holiness of your bones
the spirit that fled in death, only
to claim a larger subtler scope.
You could heal us; even such blindness
as makes night of day—as names the day night.

Heal us Jesuits; the overly content, the malcontent,
the skilled and sere of heart, the secret weepers,
the self-defeated, the defaulters, the proud of place
drinking the empty wind of honor. Help the workhorses
slow, speed the laggards, give back to routine and rote
their lost soul.
Institution, constitution, order, law—O
kiss the dead awake!
Your holy Spirit, come!

Portrait of the Artist as a Young Dolt. The gentleman has his first big space voyage among the stars. He appears not so much inflated, as utterly distracted. Lost in a part? At least apart from us, and certainly apart from courtesies, especially with the women, among whom he tries this and that ploy, pitiful, vainglorious. At table he is incapable of following any subject not initiated by himself. He offers banalities with a lofty, world-weary air, as though they were original gems worthy of the immortals.

He picks up my copy of Pascal and leafs through it in semiconscious contempt for the proceedings around the table. And he loves in my presence to refer to "women I've slept with," as though I give the slightest damn. Or he announces, always to a third party, that he "hasn't been near a church in years." Now am I supposed to supplicate or wring my hands, or what? Not knowing what to do, I hold my tongue.

Noon Mass in a side chapel of the cathedral. At the Communion, I thought of all our dear ones: Jonah House, Syracuse, Providence, Maryland, and of all in prison—Alderson, Danbury, Atlanta—and most of all, and hardest to bear, the four sent up for the atrocious sentences in Kansas City. I prayed that the grace of God would dwell in the prisoners as courage and steadfastness.

When I first met Jeremy in New York, he was departing for a transatlantic trundle, New York to London and back. He impressed me as a conventional actor, highly skilled but without notable soul. A professional in sum, in a profession that calls soul by the name skill and knows no better. Since then, especially since arriving here, he's come on something better. The "better" I call attentiveness to one's own spirit, its urgencies and appetites.

He was like a prisoner languishing behind bars, spoken to by one of those dreadful hirelings, a "court appointed lawyer" who knows nothing of the prisoner's cause or merit and cares less. The lawyer argues languidly in the public forum, windily (always with the prevailing wind), and gets paid for it. This is known cynically as "the game."

Then something happened. The prisoner is summoned forth, and he speaks for himself. It is a voice of considerable spirit; each of its seven strings comes taut, comes alive. Needless to say, in our story there follows both acquittal, restoration, and great honors.

Someone asked me in puzzlement, "What do you do in the film?"

"Let's put it this way. I'm a kind of sacred drone. I hum along with things, in extraterrestrial approbation. But when the humming stops, watch out!"

I've named one actor our Kosher Kornukopia. He's perpetually thoughtful of others and offering unexpected gifts, with panache and much patter, to be sure. Soon after our arrival, he improved the supper scene by rising, silencing us with a mighty wave of his arm, and drawing from his apparently bottomless trove, like a dark fistful of spaghetti, a clutch of wristwatches. He yelled, "One each for the boys, two each for the girls!" This was variously received.

Another actor: "The great dangers of this work are boredom and depression. You're either filming and all keyed up for it, or you're doing nothing while others are jumping through their hoops. It's the idleness that gets to you."

Sorting through the days, I discover patches of depression but not a second of boredom, so I dunno. Maybe it's because I've made good friends and read and write and meditate much; checks and balances, so to speak.

Friday, April 19. We're on the prowl for a better ending for the film than the one provided by Robert Bolt's script. The spirit of Joffé and the producer, Puttnam, is by no means hidebound, as though what was once writ was writ in stone. The point is a practical one: "Will it work?" We're puzzling over that one. And the outcome, whatever form it will take, will be a measure of ourselves as well.

In this regard, I'm reflecting at length on episodes from my checkered past. I'm thinking of the crisis in Selma, Alabama: the scene in that bare little chapel, the congregation, surrounded by the pistol-packing sheriff, his dogs and minions, the people within singing their hearts out. Dr. King's thunderous preaching. Then the question: "Do we march?" And out we streamed to face it all.

Then the great dictum of King, which we're still pondering, some twenty years later: "The church is the place you go from . . ."

*   *   *

The British class system couldn't be more vividly illustrated
than here. We have the navvies who move and heft and hammer
and climb ladders and generally knock the images together,
then knock them apart again. In the tropical clime, they wear
khaki shorts and gold chains and nothing else. Then we have
the "big boys," in jeans and corduroys and plain, long-sleeved
cotton shirts. They concoct the images, do the head work, and
start and stop things short.

Two hours were spent preparing the gigantic lights above a
garden wall. This is a quite typical effort; it will eventually be
syncopated in a two-minute scene involving three mortals. Like
a ton of rose petals distilled in a vial of perfume? One hopes the
comparison is not totally ridiculous . . .

A wave of depression washes over the actors as they finish
a stint and pass a few days or even a week in comparative
idleness. The word is of course a clue to the malaise. Once the
act is done, the mind goes slack. But I think the law of the
mind is being violated here. Idleness is the bane; the mind is
refreshed in testing and trying new rhythms, not in abandoning its powers.

It's as though one were to say: "This morning I observed
such and such on the beach or overheard such and such in
conversation. In consequence, this thought or analogy or contrast or conclusion or objection occurs to me. I'll proceed to test
it out, write it down, mull it over—or reject it out of hand. Or
I'll argue it to a draw." In any case, the mind goes, like an eye
on a pivot, from seeing this to seeing that, from blinking to
closure to opening. But it never allows that its function is a

flight from "the things seen" in the broadest sense. Or so I understand it.

At the catering tent the class system has its finest hour. The workers clot together; the cockney lingo is loud, the laughter hearty. The talking heads sit a little apart, confabulating life and death matters. The rest of us rock uneasily about, settling where we may, migrating fowl on new terrain. Our fate is being woven by other powers than ours.

The cameraman thinks only of his machine, its function, placing, focus, switch. He stands or sits on his platform, moving the great orb about ponderously, a lesser god monitoring a greater. Meantime the actor thinks only of his part; there is, according to his fiction, no eye upon him. His own eye has buried itself in dreams, like a bird of paradise asleep; and therefore in its dream most acutely awake. His soul is sewn, as his frame is, into a costume; within it, life is savage, extravagant, or slowly and somberly flowing.

Then it is done, the Big Eye turns off indifferently; it has seen all it is pleased to see. The actor collapses in a canvas chair; he is once more a mere mortal.

And now, both workman and actor are bored. The hands that held aloft a world of light and judgment and cunning invention hang lax or drum a feeble beat of monotony. Time, they say, hangs heavy on their hands.

Saturday, April 20. News of absolutely no moment. The little clock in my room squeaked once and died. It was like the demise of a mouse miming the death of a mountain. But I stuck the windstem with a bit of scotch tape and the creature perked

up and held firm; it is still chirping away its inner coherence
with the mighty planets.

The political and religious understanding of the actors is
quite uneven, I would judge, with the women far ahead of the
men. I talk of Greenham Common and our people in prison and
describe our actions and discuss nonviolence, and the women
nod with understanding while the men glance past or nervously
light up a smoke.

And yet, and yet. The task we set ourselves in the film is,
rightly understood, all but beyond rational powers. The actors
(men all) are attempting something audacious, miming the in-
candescent spirits of Jesuits who blazed a path through the
eighteenth-century jungle of ignorance, lust, and avarice, and
who created so splendid a utopia, on behalf of others, that one
still gasps for wonderment.

We're roughly in the same situation in things religious.
There's great ignorance of something once referred to as a
viable tradition. The actors know little about God or prayer or
sacraments or the church—or the Jesuits, for that matter. They
cast an outsider's (i.e., a performer's) look on the pope, give him
a tribute of sorts, as being an outstanding member of the club—
a "great performer,"—a tribute which, to my mind, is ambigu-
ous in the extreme.

And yet, they're girding to take the part of "contemplatives
in action," who brought ancient symbols into dangerous places
and there won a glory beyond measure, even as they were
bringing to the symbols an unexampled newness and vitality.
They created biblical "new cities," brought new skills and com-
prehensions and utter courage to bear on the tragic fate of the

Indians. They combated dishonor, distemper, and the disincarnate, so-called faith of Christians who had renounced all recognizable claim to that title.

It would be difficult to imagine a greater disparity: the lives of the actors on the one hand (including my own) and the lives of those portrayed.

I know little of that invisible point at which our pampered skills can touch the strings and gut of things and raise the solemn basso of very soul.

The actors from time to time will describe their homes, and one can guess their income; there are no more favored children of the dream. Theirs is a style of elegant understatement, sure of itself, securely in possession.

I feel neither emulation nor awe as I move in such company; their undoubted skills leave me not cold, but cool. Perhaps there is a kind of achieved humility we may learn from one another.

And beyond doubt, thrown together as we are from two continents upon the shores of a third, we already bear a tender affection for one another.

Sunday, April 21. We assemble in the old city, in the courtyard of Roland's home. "You are the film." Roland offers the actors a brief ferverino. He urges us to mingle, take meals together, and so on.

But if we are the film, what of him? Guiding spirit? Bearer of good news, holy and secular? Encourager? Wiper away of tears? Stern exactor? Friend? Father confessor? All and any. Indeed, he appears to me at times as the only authentic Jesuit of us all.

* * *

Yesterday marked the entrance of his Malevolent Munificence, Mendoza, into the square. They boarded up the statue of Columbus in the middle. Thus with a snap of finger and a falling hammer did Cartagena become Asunción.

Flourish of sleeve and glove, advance and recession and feint of beauties at the high windows, feline and provocative. Slaves by the naked score. Slaves yoked, roped together, running behind the thoroughbreds. Glory, dishonor, sin, wretchedness, willfulness, church and state in proud sovereignty and mutuality. A horror to the mind, knowing as one does where such a procession must lead, as a matter of their future and our dolorous history.

Savage, splendid, top-heavy headdresses and masks of wicker and cunning, dovetailed feathers. Palanquins of saints, native and foreign; saints of the city, the countryside; ancient martyrs, their wounds gaping. Bishops, humble layfolk. Virgins rolling their eyes excessively to heaven. Saints who were laborers on earth, bearing square and compass, rule and sextant.

And in the midst of the celestial entourage, stark hands and face visible beneath her garments of sorrow, the Black Virgin. The other hierophants are a simple fiction; only she is real. A living maiden! No paint or plaster, it is inferred, could do justice to such a personage; Mother of God, Mother of Sorrows.

She lies at the heart of all fictions, their deepest truth; others may mime life; she is herself, and living. And what mere doll, accoutered and painted like a bird of paradise, could mime the life that radiates from this being? She trembles precariously there on her trestle, floating between heaven and earth, between grace and gravity. Her color, according to the canons of Spanish baroque, are expressive of the dark night of the soul. Seven daggers pierce her heart; her grief is beyond assuaging. Handmaid of the religious logic that flourished among slaveholders, the Virgin is blind. More; she strikes the procession blind as well. Her sorrows are wrapped within; she is ignorant as the dead of the sorrows of the slaves who bring up the rear of her procession.

Slave traders, mercenaries, settlers, together with a complaisant church, these have frozen her in an icy block of time. Her sorrows are a matter of ages past, the stuff of taxidermy and of taxidermic religion. The will that created her image, the hands that placed her here forbid her to raise her eyes to the living who groan in her wake. She cannot so much as turn her head to witness the sale and indenture of human flesh.

Thus are divine realities made serviceable to inhuman ends. The procession is conceived as a living organism. Color must balance and contrast nicely, the play of splendor be both intense and subtle, from highest to lowest, from the living Virgin to the living slaves.

But what they cannot understand, these blind artificers, is that God has cut the snake in two; the hindquarters have escaped the bonds and whips. The snake is healed and abroad, and venomously bent on retribution. In our century.

Not to neglect another point—the Virgin also is liberated. The doll has cast off the doll clothes; the woman has cast off the doll mask, the useless limbs. She is no longer a deaf-mute in service to the powerful. She flees the palanquin and mingles with the disenfranchised, the wretched of the earth. In every colonial plaza and sanctuary, at midnight you may hear this Cassandra: "God has exalted the slaves . . . has sent the proud away empty . . . has filled the hungry with good things . . ." The slaves hear her voice.

*   *   *

When I came here to help make a movie, I had a strong sense that my best understanding would be it's all for the fun of it. And when I put together a book, especially a book of poetry, it is the same. But when I try to live in the way I am called to live, that becomes serious indeed.

Even then, I notice that my best foot (the third one) inches its way forward. When I'm at my best (my least worst), the fun tends to take over. It all becomes celebration, even on the dung heap.

And when nature comes beating at my shores, as now, and blazes a blessing from on high (as now) I sense the heart of it all is celebration.

Then there rises that gravelly voice of reproof, as though it groaned from the everlasting pit, "But how can you dare celebrate in such a world? Are you no more than a frivolous parasite, feeding off the anguish of others?"

I have no answer. But I know the opposite landscape of the fiesta is that pit, and I have all but gone under. My family and a few friends know this, and they never venture on a question like the one above.

Can the king's confessor call the king to an accounting? The question does not arise directly in the film, but it hovers overhead, a cloud no bigger than a hand. Because Père de la Chaise and other powerful Jesuits had the king's ear and were able to appeal to his better part the sword poised over the mission was stayed. But only for a time. King Henry had a worse part as well as a better, as his letter to the pope shows. And the worse prevailed.

The Jesuits, along with their works, the culture they had built for one hundred and fifty laborious years out of Indian despair and burgeoning hope, their neophytes and ample farms and flourishing trade, the liturgy and music—all the complex simplicity of great achievement—all were crushed.

That "worse part" of the king was compounded of avarice and envy, ego and cruelty. Many hands compounded the poison. Presently, the king tasted the brew, and approved it. *Pereant!*

Minimal expectations versus maximal. I would pray at least not to be ashamed of what we produce here. That same sense of shame makes me rail against yet another bedroom scene, that climacteric and cliché. But I am offered this explanation: the fratricide that follows must be so explained, a brother grown furious because his brother has won the lady's heart.

I said there were other reasons than failed love to turn on one another.

They countered that, ah, but those other reasons were not so easy to show quickly on the screen.

So I conclude that we have settled for the fast fix, since to explore those other reasons and their images would require considerable outlay of imagination, and therefore cause delay.

So it is decreed; we shall have our bedroom scene. Actually we could rent the footage cheap; it sits in film archives in a thousand canisters marked "Boredom, bedroom."

Pascal says of the Jesuits: "These people [sic] corrupt the laws; the model is spoiled." Good Jansenist as he was, he had no respect for those who were undergoing testing and discerning in a most unspiritual world. It can at least be claimed for the Jesuits that they took their chances in the midst of those incapable alike of distinguishing in moral matters and of heroism in the same matters. Pascal had a point; but his pride led him to widen its circumference until every Jesuit should be included and disposed of. This was unjust, and a counter-casuistry to boot—"Be like me or be damned." But if all Jesuits, say, had been converted to Jansenism, who would be saved? And how to choose between a Jesuit hell and a Jansenist heaven each conducted by Jansenists? A rock and a hard place indeed!

Something ungenerous and chilling in him. Qualities to be avoided in the film, as (I would venture) they were absent in the Jesuits. But what sort of community did Pascal dwell in? Ungenerous, chilling? He may well have encountered the kind of Jesuit who would awaken only scorn. So have I. But by what right does one generalize? Pascal must have heard of Ignatius, Peter Favre, Xavier, and so many others of stature and integrity. And for every pampered "Jesuit de salon," every hair-splitting casuist, there were (and are) hundreds who live in austere circumstances, many in self-chosen exile on the missions. Many martyred for the faith their adversary accused them of betraying. Pascal knew this, but he chose not to know. Hence his bile runs free; he displays it under an unassailable rhetoric: "Those who love the church must condemn the Jesuits."

If we but knew the world! Such knowledge would be our salvation—or our damnation. Mendoza rides into Asunción; a tide of misery follows captive at his heels. He looks straight ahead, steely, self-possessed. And hell is in his wake, and he is responsible. Except that up to this point, he does not know it.

How can he not know it? Easily such blindness is the simplest thing in the world. Ignorance of one's moral state is in fact the hellish fuel that makes the world go round.

One thinks of Mendoza, then of the Satan of *Paradise Lost.* It is an incomplete description of such entities to call them self-damned. The state of Satan, at least, is worse; he is the spoiled model of things, the Antichrist. He is also the *motor mundi*; he greases the gears, he revs things up. And Mendoza is the exquisitely tuned image of the spoiled image. Filthy lucre, immaculate hands. Blindest of the blind.

The script is to the finished film as a skeleton to a living body in its world. Imagination fleshes things in. But what if, in the first place, the skeleton is fused, immobile? Or if it contains here a twisted bone, there a disc badly aligned? Then one must say to the creator, "I pray you, start over. With all due respect, you've botched things."

A few of us talked at length of what Bill Lynch calls the "magniloquent imagination," a sickness of spirit deep and wild, ubiquitous and assaulting, in the media and cinema. I confessed to a native, perhaps naive preference for black and white photos, old film classics (precolor), modest films, in which the fate of the human, realized step by step, might illuminate the life of the beholder.

It was of interest that several in the group, including myself, confessed to being beaten about mercilessly by the images of *The Killing Fields.*

What comes of it all? Another instance in which massive horror has become the texture of life itself? Depleted emotions? Numbed purpose? A sense of hopelessness, I thought, can only ensure that crime will repeat itself, since only a furious, aroused, and disciplined citizenry can stand in the way . . .

Are we serving to an already glutted public no more than the bread and circuses of empire? Will *The Mission* do more than further stupefy a sluggish people already in lockstep? What finally is the point of the whole thing?

Fully nine-tenths of the current film offerings, to judge them charitably, are either at odds with the health of the mind or are of no significance one way or another: Free Day in the Fun House. What then of *The Mission*? Its grandiosities can easily swamp the best efforts of its leading actors, humans whose choices place them in opposing fields of force, testing their human fiber and fidelity. Are not these the point, the only justification of this immense effort?

The deep-dyed villain of our artifice came to me somewhat in secret, somewhat like Nicodemus in the Gospel. He is cut out by nature if not by art, to play a rich, unconscionable slave trader. But if ever heart belied face, it is this one. He came with a plan—to gather all the leftover food from the staff tent and the hotel, transport it to the barrio, and feed the multitudes of underfed children. I am considered an ally in this, since I have already visited the neighborhood and seen the misery there.

Five women continue to administer and teach at the barrio school, even though evicted from their order for daring so Christian an impertinence. So we'll start with the sisters, and see how things develop.

But to speak of our friend, how had he come upon his purpose? He reported he had seen an old man foraging in a garbage can outside a restaurant where he had just consumed a fifty-dollar dinner. He was unable to sleep that night; toward dawn the plan occurred to him.

Now I suppose many a luminary, here and almost anywhere in the world, has witnessed a scene of misery such as our friend described. But who will be affected to the point of moving a little superfluous wealth and removing thereby a little superfluous hunger?

I read that the eighteenth-century Portuguese hired large numbers of mercenaries to invade the missions, to disrupt, murder, and lead Indians off into slavery. They even disguised some of their number as Jesuits to further confuse matters; thus the Indians could have been led to believe that the missioners' purpose was only to betray them to their enemies. Of course the attacks were illegal, since the missions were under the direct protection of the king . . .

It struck me that the "contras" presently ravaging Nicaragua are a very old idea. When one is inclined to wage war, both illegally and contrary to popular will, he simply goes ahead in secrecy, under cover of lies, and pays for murder as he goes.

Roland looks exhausted after four weeks here. But then he looked little different in New York before all this turmoil got underway. Most love him; all, even the grudging, respect him; more than should do so, lean on him.

As for De Niro, the star seems many light-years distant, somewhat as though his entire existence and personality have passed into the film, as though for the duration his life will be available only to the camera and the director. This is a hard vocation, also, if the term makes any sense, a notable asceticism.

If I were to inquire of myself in Shakespeare's day, "What is the point of such and such a play?" I might come on a moment of quite startling clarity. "I must see life, my life, in such and such a mirror, even in a greviously distorted mirror like Iago or Richard, before I can hope to understand my life." Or "I thought that to a point I was facing up to life and death. And then I saw and heard Hamlet and was led a step further, primarily in understanding and secondarily (and more problematically) in action—a new mode of action or an intensified mode of action . . ." A passion is generated in the audience, at least in some of the audience, analogous to the passion that first generated the play.

But of what are we made capable (or more capable, or at least less incapable) by the common run of today's films or, for that matter, today's stage? Commonly, I submit, they amount to a perverse celebration of infirmity and incapacity. The human is throttled, slowly or speedily. Death is gloried in. The glory is spectacle, expenditure on a grand scale, technique gone wild, trickery and quackery, the shortcut of violence.

The modes of death are infinitely inventive, a series of images, befallings, jokes, crises, the sum of which seems to be this: that the world's business, as presently conducted, is not at all intolerable. Or another extreme: that same world to those capable of "realism" is unmanageably beyond recall or direction. In consequence, skills of the human had best be restrained to mutual stroking and solacing—of a few by a few. Attempts at further outreach, resistance, political responsibility, it is suggested, are a plain waste.

Do the films merely follow the cultural drift, mirroring it to little avail? One thing seems certain: very few are capable of offering a contrary vision.

One thinks of the gradual contraction of the human in Bergman's films. They started with a stunning mythological search, through long reaches of history, for meaning, for God, for symbols that might illumine the human predicament. And they offer us, of late years, chic Swedish living rooms, where a modern couple occupy themselves in psychologically rending one another limb from limb.

Some things are almost too painful to recount—and no fiction either! On Sunday, as I sat reading on the beach, my sack was stolen, and all the chattels therein. And today, as I promenaded homeward from the old city, a big blustery fellow approached. He was either angry or mad or a touch of both. With many a black look he demanded pesos—or else. At a loss, I proceeded toward the street adjacent to the beach, seeking help. And lo, salvation! A cop was lounging about there.

Our friend, quick to seize whatever advantage, ran ahead of me and began violently expostulating with the law, something to the effect that I had stolen his money, no less. The law took things calmly, greeted me equably, and asked to view the contents of my bag. Finding nothing of note, the cop turned about, confronted the sullen interloper, and advised him to get lost pronto, which he did, a shambles of misery and smoldering anger. And I was left to wonder at the abysmal defeats that produce such conduct. And was saddened by the thought.

My Jesuit companero here is much attached to the Mass kit and the Ignatian *Letter on Obedience* and the *Rules of the Order.* Alas, he also gravitates in conversation to various violent anecdotes that have stuck in his craw, like irritants he regards as veritable pearls. The Mass, the Law, and then Jesus!— a kind of Galloping Ghost through history, firing up the troops.

I have no such images and resources to comfort me, only a question. What form does that version of the human yclept Christian take, given such days as we must endure? To put flesh on the galloping ghost is only to succeed in unhorsing the holy. The task, I believe, is quite other—to strip our gods of horse and lance, which is to say, of our compulsions and ponderous obsessions, our distended appetite for power, our slavery to ego, our hedonistic clutch on "the things which are seen." Such gods, such possessive demons! To strip the gods is to submit to our own exorcism. Each and all, and gradually, and with great patience.

*   *   *

"For God so loved the world as to give his only Son . . . Not to judge, but to save . . ." In pondering such words, I have a sense that I am hearing within the noiseless movement of all things, the movement of the bones of the universe in their sockets. Or as though Jonah within the whale were pumping the great mammal through the deep. As though he were the heart of the whale. To act in accord with this love . . .

"Let us define the limits" (Pascal).
"They forgot to be modest, that was all" (Camus).

Thursday, April 25. Two young Jesuits, Francisco and Antonio, welcomed a group of us thespians to the barrio of Cartagena. I'm moved beyond words when I encounter Jesuits who live and work in the midst of the poor. These two seem to embody an ancient report sent to Jesuit headquarters regarding the first missioners of the Order to reach the Paraguayan jungle in 1590: "Having little or nothing, eating little and sleeping less, much given to prayer and favored by God, very close to one another in the bonds of love."

The visit was one of the best things that could have happened to us. We were, I judge, encountering Jesuits of the quality of those we are trying to portray with a measure of fidelity. All of us went home a bit more sobered than we came.

Is it possible to live the style favored by these ornaments of the firmament, our film stars, and still utter noble sentiments elegantly? It seems one thing to play a part, with brilliance and verisimilitude, quite another to unite one's heroic alter ego with personal convictions.

If such inner unity held firm, an interesting question arises:

would we be here at all? Or if here, disporting ourselves at the Hilton? Padre Antonio, one of the Jesuits of the barrio, confessed that on first hearing our wish to visit him and his people, he felt in no way inclined to welcome us. Making a posh film in the midst of the misery of Colombia, rolling back the past with such expense and exactness—are we anything more than necrophiliacs?

The workdays are such that we have little or no time even to raise the question. Or so we judge.

A manifestly irrational idea follows; to wit, in serious matters, humans are inclined to act rationally.

Thus with regard to the subject of the movie, an overriding "rational" supposition would go something like: a Christian people, the Spanish, its ships nosing about the edges of the world, would undoubtedly win the hearts and minds of the indigenous peoples they came on. Spontaneous acceptance of the newcomers would be inevitable, given (rationally) the purity of life, freedom from avarice, lust, and ambition of the European arrivals. There would be no conceivable need for establishing fortified remote towns for endangered natives. Of course. Quite to the contrary. The continent of transported Europeans and Indians would be transformed in a single generation into a seemly, modest, hardworking, celebratory utopia under the benediction of God, the pope, the king, and the Jesuits.

Let us go further in our rational quest. This political and religious triumph, a New World indeed, would become a world model. Its vitality would overflow into all areas where explorations were destroying old social forms and creating new ones. By a marvelous spontaneous generation, similar ideal societies would begin to arise around the world.

Homo homini lupus? Inconceivable! Indeed, a new motto is forged for the escutcheon of the race of humans: *Homo homini agnus.*

Alas for "rationality," that ideal so essentially romantic, illiterate of the meaning of original sin, blind to the darkness of the human heart! The real world offers a different evidence; utopias rarely come into being, lead for their duration an always endangered existence, and then perish.

The Paraguayan "reducciónes" began, it is worth noting, not through the romantic confabulations of Rousseau, or the theories of Taine, or pre-Marxian analysis. There was an altogether lucky conjunction of two factors, neither of which could have been arbitrarily created. The first was the humanism of the Jesuits, their sensible and compassionate tradition; in its purest form, it owes everything to the "gospel of the underdog," to which the Jesuits were strangely and inordinately attached. Then there was the limitless wilderness to which they could flee, the victimized and the Jesuits . . .

"Orders" for the day following arrive mysteriously and are deposited at one's door each evening. I think nostalgically of the old-fashioned commands of the novitiate, when without ado or palaver one was dispatched to this or that pilgrimage, chore, or change of locale. No questions were asked (or answered if asked); there was none of the current piffle of "dialogue" or "discernment." This is like that.

News of absolutely no moment. As we lined up to board Avianca Airlines for Santa Rosa, the wife of the Dutch ambassador greeted us. She was carrying in her arms a truly wondrous specimen, a sloth. She and her burden quite stopped the show.

The creature clung to her like the newborn; its head turned ever so slowly over her shoulder, regarding us with mild wonderment. The great arms and legs were covered with the softest silvery fur. It looked out on the world, blinking slowly, as though clearing cobwebs from the mind, or as though it could scarcely credit what it saw, this world of nonsloths walking rapidly into the rear end of an iron bird.

I am aloft, the sloth and I. In some century to come, it will be told ever so s-l-o-w-l-y around a sloth campfire, how once upon a Cartagena morning a sloth flew like a shot arrow through incalculable space . . .

Four of us held a discussion at the airport. Who of our own day were entitled to be named the lawful descendants of the Jesuits we portray in the film? We conjured up a noble gallery, from the priests we met in the barrios of Cartagena, to explorers, climbers of Mt. Everest, to space walkers. And then came the conscientious heroes and martyrs, Dr. King, Gandhi, and the "cloud of witnesses" of our century.

I suggested the unfinished business of the planet could be understood as the bloody vortex of the human scene itself; for my part, the work of unity and justice lagged terribly behind the rage for technique or geographical exploration; we were in fact squatting on our turf like illiterate, benumbed cave folk, while a nuclear night rumbled its thunders outside. I said that in such a fix I had become aware, perforce, of a religious possibility—the power of creating dramatic symbols that might help the cave people issue from the cave. On the walls of the cave, by the way, were traced images of torpor and helplessness that kept the denizens terrified or morally off balance, images (media?) purporting to announce "the news," events transpiring outside the cave. They were something other; images of chicanery and befuddlement, of bloodthirst and ferocity. They were offered in stupefying variety (but were always strangely alike). They purported to offer the sum total of human capacity.

"They mistood the images for reality" (Plato).

Is our film creating better images, symbols, rhythms, truths embodied? Is it apt to persuade the captives that they can come forth, that even the "first death" (Revelation) outside is preferable to the "second death," inertia, helplessness, captivity in the cave?

For the first time, I find myself among the extraordinary aboriginal folk who were transported here, some three hundred and fifty miles by air, to inhabit a village built for them and work with us in the mission sequence as it develops.

A VISIT TO THE ONANI INDIANS

You dwell lifelong in a jungle clearing
A hut, a plank porch, yourself, and
the vast gangrenous green, proliferating
far as the encircled eyes' round.
Then you'd better create poetry!
It's not over and above, it's plain survival.
(An Indian, a prisoner knows)
Like a plumed sun in high style
You sway, pound the earth in praise;
Your paint proclaiming wilful bodily joy
and the drums speak for you, the flutes.

O the dance, the stifled heart
set free
the vowels of birds in a vocal reed,
the body's splendor,
the momentary lost and found
blaze of the human!

We went upriver to view the last stages of construction of Father Gabriel's mission, including the church, the dwelling of the priests, refectory, Indian workshops, and so on. Then we waded downstream at the invitation of the Indians, while they climbed trees hunting iguanas. They brought down five of these astonishing reptiles and bore them proudly homeward, one hand grasping the tail, the other the fearsome head. The reptile, unpalatable and scaly as it appears, forms an entrée, we were told, much prized.

Tonight in the village, an international soccer match has captured all attention. A television is set in the midst of the open-sided shelter where folks eat and recreate. The place is lively indeed with banter and combat, as favorite teams are celebrated and opponents vigorously put down. Many of the men are sporting MISSION T-shirts. These, I understand, were a gift from the film company—a gift with strings. The women, who normally (as here and now) go about naked above the waist, were invited to don this chic finery while traveling from their village to Santa Marta. A protection no doubt.

I met the shaman, a magnificent old man with a teak face, a mask of Buddhist beatitude. He carved a series of sticks, that lie in a basket above the door of one of the dwellings. I am told various healing powers are associated with these.

I was also told of a delicious happening in our instant village. It appears that the keeper of the granary, a Colombian, informed the shaman that he was determined to exterminate a colony of mice who were encroaching on the foodstuffs of the community. The shaman anxiously asked if he would please hold off until he could consult with the mice, which, according to the account, he proceeded to do. He returned after a period to report bad news and good. The bad news was that the mice refused to depart. They had occupied the place longer than humans (so their message went); moreover, they had literally no place to go. The good was that they would accept all prohibitions, honor bound. The storekeeper grew severe, even in concessions, but he agreed to withhold the minislaughter, as long as the mice observed the covenant.

The story has a happy ending, as such delightful doings must. To the hour of recounting, there was not the slightest minilarceny. The mice rustle about discreetly in the palm roof, commerce goes its merry way beneath.

What will be the future of the Indians, these innocent and wondrous beings, whose kindness extends to all the living, to colonies of mice, even to us, who, when one remembers the extermination policy of colonial history, have the least claim on their clemency? Ricardo, the Colombian who oversaw their transfer here, grants a mere forty or fifty years, until they become assimilated into the worldwide homogeny of education, technique, and money getting.

In consenting to travel to Santa Marta, the Indians have landed in the world for the first time. A truly awesome thought. They have arrived in our world, which goes by the presumptive name of the real world. One can only glance at the radiant faces and breathe a prayer. God help them.

They also entered the economy when they came here; perhaps that says it all, "real" and "world" and more. The arrangement is that families will be paid two-thirds of the stipulated salary; the remaining third goes into a communal fund for education and medical needs.

About 9:30 one night a violent tropical storm broke out, a brisk reminder that we're in the midst of the rainy season.

Luckily all dwellings are roofed in tin under their thatch. As to their weatherproof quality, we shall have a chance to test it, perhaps to our chagrined liquefaction, tonight . . . A few hardy souls are abroad, braving the storm, checking on the functioning of drainage ditches.

Saturday, April 27. The eighteenth-century missioners reported home, among other wondrous items, the following: the most efficacious way to repel a charging tiger was to piss in its eye. Such a feat, if ever in fact accomplished, introduces a few intriguing questions perhaps best left unasked here.

Slept last night in a lumpy cot, having eschewed the hammock as lethal to my aching back. The rain made a resonant rat-a-tat on the tin roof. Slept soundly, dreamed spectacularly; but like the child's dream of Ali Baba's cave, lost it all on awakening.

On each Indian dwelling here is painted a bright band of a different color, an ingenious way of ensuring easy identification of one's house, especially, I am told, since counting is not among their skills.

Sunday, April 28. On awakening, we enjoyed three hours of the most beautiful and diverse dancing. At the start, shortly after dawn, a hollowed canoe became a booming drum, its prow suspended and slightly tipped upward toward the east. An elderly woman stood there, staring fixedly toward the dawn, beating weightily and steadily. Gradually, a circle of women formed about her, some bearing infants, a few pregnant, others leading small children by the hand. They shuffled and shimmied along in a simple two-step.

Outside the women's circle, five or six men moved in a tight knot to the same rhythm, blowing flutes and whistles. Two of the flutes were fully six feet long; given the limited space and the crowd of onlookers, these instruments were managed with great skill.

We breakfasted on hot sweet coffee, french fries, and wedges of fresh pineapple. These seemingly incompatible comestibles went down peacefully enough—and stayed down, despite all gloomy prognostications and rumblings.

Last night's rain fell for hours, memorably. It burst the cloudy night like a wet sack spilling. I ventured a walk in an interval between rounds of deluge. At the edge of our clearing, a massive low-lying tree was lit by a swarm of fireflies like a black peacock. It was a Christmas Eve out of due season.

Then with the rain the ground sprouted, sudden as fungi, with frogs. Presently their entire orchestra struck up, bass to treble.

Among the Indians, men and women conduct themselves according to a classic pattern. Men and boys tend to bilingual skills, Onani and Spanish, mainly due to the village TV at home. Younger men have a jaunty, slightly askew, worldly air; here and there an unlikely T-shirt celebrates faery lands forlorn, Miami or such. No frippery for the women—traditional beads and sarongs. In the evening, the men hover above the chess-boards or slap down their dominoes with mucho gusto. The women meantime sit about inconspicuously on their heels, weaving rushes with flying fingers; they say little, even to one another; and the children flock around them, but quietly, quietly.

The iguanas that fell ingloriously from high trees yesterday and were captured and dragged home in triumph have disappeared, every one, into the pots of individual families.

Perhaps a sublime dislocation of spirit brought on by my dwelling for a time with the Indians induced what follows. In any case, here goes.

I suddenly sensed the ego as a conscious bowl or vessel, which had emptied, was void as a concave mirror under an empty sky. The only thought of this thinking vessel, which was all one, was of hunger, hunger to be filled once more with self, at all cost, under whatever guise.

The empty sky, which the vessel reflected (and to that degree possessed) was not enough. For the sky too was empty and therefore of no avail. What was hungered for was a bowlful of images, like a *fruit de mare*, images of everything living, a plethora of images, mixed with a savory sauce that was their second nature and element.

Now the meal was underway, and I thought the second state of the bowl, its fullness, was worse than the first—a kind of second death. For if the ego consumed the images, it became the images, and their helter-skelter incoherence. The soul was filled with "the things which are seen." One became a "dweller on the earth," in the awful judgment of Revelation. Stuck in the world up to one's neck, like Beckett's victims, unable to imagine another world beyond the glutted ego.

(Still I must take care not to be possessed by the superhuman, even while imagining the superhuman, which is to say, the damned.)

Enough of images, our plight. But where is our healing?

I must keep tipping the bowl over, since left to itself, it keeps filling up.

What is the point, it cries, of an empty vessel, a void? What could be thought more useless under the sun (that analogate of fullness and life), or on earth, or on the moon, that has the grace of humility and impoverishment, whose bowl is a begging bowl?

I considered like a bearded Ecclesiastes all things under the sun and the sun itself. And I concluded, rashly no doubt: it is for you, despite all, to live as a counterimage. Where there is bursting fullness, be empty. Where there is anger, forgive. Where perversity, be childlike. Where there is muscle and rampageous power, play the idiot, the inarticulate . . .

We are making a film about Jesuits who were, in principle and discipline, empty vessels, passionately in, and just as passionately not of, the world. We who imagine the film are veritably moving mountains, workers, artifacts, costumes, Europeans and Americans and idigenous peoples—all to create a coherent sequence of images and counterimages, power and helplessness, faith and betrayal, complicity and innocence. The meeting of these, the collision, the ricochet, and destruction.

Anything remotely resembling the Resurrection must wait. It lies somewhere in the darkness offstage, a matter of hope. It can only be remotely glimpsed in the lives and deaths of the Indians and the Jesuits, their steadfastness, their love for one another even unto death.

The images question history (and land at our doorstep) with a sublime *simpático* for the victims. They probe the dark side of the splendid Spanish moon (and our moon) . . .

Then I saw two caves. One was a workshop, the other a dwelling. The first resounds with the controlled frenzy of Vulcan; in it, the accoutrements of war and power are being forged.

The second is modest. It is barely large enough for one inhabitant, possibly two. As to its current inhabitant, he could best be described as an empty vessel. To great enterprises, he is very nearly useless, inefficient. He has no discernable goals.

Like a child or a mentally disabled person, he speaks seldom, usually when spoken to. He keeps a certain distance from the clamor and beat of the great world, a distance best understood as a silent skepticism. Yet it would be inaccurate not to add that he radiates a kind of aura.

Now and again the vulcanizers of time and this world discover this other cave (which might almost be thought of as another world). They seek out this strange specimen, if only to be silent for an hour or two, perhaps out of hunger for different images or for a place empty of all images.

They return to their blazing forge with second thoughts, thoughts greatly different from their first ones, for the bowl of our story is also the cave. And the cave is not a void but a vessel.

Mony, the Cambodian actor, and I were talking over coffee. Subject: actors and acting. It seemed to us that one among our companeros had discovered who he was and, in consequence, was resisting colonization-by-media. Another seemed quite unsure of himself and (as I described him) kept appearing just this side of the mirror, then disappearing into it. Just short of being himself, he operated at a thin silver edge of appearance, of mime and put-on.

I venture that in many ways our Jesuit novitiate could be understood as an actors' school. We were closely instructed and monitored in costume and conduct. We were to be sober, restrained, and skilled in something known as a "spiritual vocabulary" (as restricted as an immigrant's or a displaced person's). We were like aliens on our own soil (and proudly so, the gospel often being invoked in support of this sense of not belonging). We were moreover to beware of something redundantly referred to as "particular friendship."

*   *   *

Unaccountably, and contrary to all common sense, we were to spurn all and any clues as to "connaturality," whether of talent or outlook or goodness or the reasons of the heart, clues from which we might infer that there stood near us an absolutely undeserved and gracious Other. That Other was of course paid tribute to; the coinage was prayer, penance, loneliness, and a cheerful mien under adversity. We were to pay and pay; it was a matter of life and death, hyphenated realities when all was said. It was a mystical ascent we were summoned to undertake out of this world; it was not merely up the seven-story mountain of Dante, but the vertical ladder of Jacob. But as to clues to the right way? They were suspect; they had led many astray.

I told of the austere elderly Jesuit once held up to us for emulation. It seemed he was approached by someone who dared say, "I met a friend of yours the other day," or some such passing remark, only to be brought up short by this soul of iron, "I have many acquaintances, but only one Friend."

The final word was so pronounced as to demand a capital letter. I was to reflect years later that the Friend so austerely invoked had, on the occasion, not been heard from.

The sound of things.

In the Indian village, if one closed eyes, there was a mysterious hum of low voices, the swish and buzz of brooms sweeping the fallen leaves, the birdlike counterpoint of the children's treble—the variety and subdued consonance of a human hive. "Pervasive," "gentle," "palpable," "energetic," "subdued"— such words occurred. I had never heard anything quite like it.

There were minor variations—the drums and flutes and pounding heels of dance. But these were only occasional, while the sweet undercurrent went on from dawn to dusk. I thought of it as a kind of undifferentiated storehouse of sound, only partially released; it was oboes and flutes, so to speak, with the great kettledrum in reserve. This was prelanguage and language, presence and sense, accompanied by body gesture and illustrated by body paint.

The only intrusive sound I heard all day was the clatter of the generator. But when this mechanical Merlin switched lights on at dusk, I could only be grateful. And at 10:00 P.M. the machine sputtered off and went to sleep.

The village is immaculately clean, as are the villagers; they bathe several times each day in the river, making of each event a kind of fiesta, everyone joking and splashing about and making great ado with the children. Nor could their sense of dignity be missed, even by the veriest lout. The women remain somewhat detached from the male bustle and hustle; they weave their wondrous baskets, nurse the infants, or even perform both chores at once.

I was idling in a hammock on someone's porch, literally drinking in the village scene. One of the children, under pretense of examining my watch, crept into the hammock with me. He and I swung and swayed together. I took joy in this skinful of eels and we laughed together nonsensically.

A Jesuit from the barrio said to me at our first meeting, "All of us in Latin America know of your work." Surely he was overgenerous, but it was a great consolation nonetheless. He must have meant, in an appreciative sense, those Jesuits who are planted among the poor until death do them part. To be known by them, and thanked, is the greatest gift I could dream of.

*   *   *

Prickly jealousies and mutually confounding egos among the actors render life interesting. The aforementioned contrarieties are compounded by sun, surf, and isolation. We have the whole range—moodiness, temper, appetite, struttings and moultings, ploys to avoid this one or gain a hearing from that. Some are pleased to play their part offstage, interminably. Some are weightily philosophic, others acerbic. Still others instruct one in the ways of the world and in making one's mark there. As though, indeed, one gave a damn.

There are two livid, ghastly parrots swinging about the garden trees of the hotel, forever crossing beaks and attempting to unseat one another, squawking and puffing their feathers to the admiring cries of the guests. In sum, they play their part, like a superfluity of ego in nature. Their antics raise a question by way of excess, to wit, when is enough, enough?

"Perfection of the life, or of the art" (Yeats). The dilemma may be unconscious, but it exists for all of that. To the eyes of the spirit, the actors are hardly without flaw, as their spouses or former spouses or friends or former friends could well testify, for some act with brilliance, and some live responsibly, but few are capable of both.

I have a sense that all but overwhelms me at times; it is desolating in the extreme. It comes when I recall the great blocks of skyscraper apartments and condos in New York, the misery the rich live off, then the disoriented homeless folk passing the great houses that cast an icy shadow. The desolation goes deeper, as it must . . . to think of human qualities used up, exhausted, given up on, our sense of one another destroyed by merciless church and war-making state.

Or an equally awful reflection—the Christian "thing" used up, the symbols empty, meaningless, formalist, a dance of marionettes. In my better moments I know this is a lie. I know that in so many places, in South Africa and Central America and in the courts and prisons at home, the bread is being broken like a great earthquake in nature and the wine poured out like a lava. Even the bishops hear the thunders and now and again drink the living wine, a wine offered not by their hands at all, but pouring out of prisons and graves. The secret springs of life are set free by the disappeared and tortured who live at the heart of that darkness we name God.

But not all partake of this. And not because some are unworthy (we are all unworthy), but because some are heedless, blind.

Came by speedboat with the other actors to Bocachica Island, where a vast scene is in progress—the blessing of the troops. The scene is one of grandiosity to the nth power. I see from the upper battlements of the fort an elegant coach and four, Roland surrounded by eager subalterns of all stripes. He leans into the window of the coach, occupied grandly by Altimirano, the papal delegate to the mission. And then he utters one of those disconcerting, brilliant remarks of his, going to the heart of matters.

"It is at this moment [a moment of purported triumph for bellicose diplomacy and therefore of triumph for this ecclesiastical grandee] that you realize your youth is over; the future has passed to other hands."

Meantime the jackasses are bellowing like a chorus of condemned camels; the assistant to the assistant director is bawling at the mercenaries; the flags stiffen. And finally the donkeys are browbeaten into silence.

The Indians stand about in the burning sun, nonchalant, splendid in body paint, their hair clotted with clay. A dominie, surrounded by reverent military, is intoning a prayer to a purported god of armies—our god against theirs. Another example of something known here and there as "the persistence of a sense of the holy"—a sentiment that would propel any thoughtful being straight into the arms of atheism.

Malfunction is my middle name. At times, I'm moved to lift two (left) hands to heaven in utmost chagrin. What cosmic joker first thought of me? Then I am consoled, but barely, thinking of Merton's long solitary sojourn as a hermit, where he seems to have unlearned all the common skills of existence. Then I think of his first voyage into the world, followed so swiftly by his journey out of it. His ineptitude extended indefinitely—even to the point of inability to stay alive. He seems to have pushed, on a certain awful day, his damp butt into an exposed wire.

Tuesday, April 30. Today is to be created the Great Pivotal Scene upon Which All Depends. Gabriel is to confront Mendoza, now become a despairing recluse after his murderous assault on his brother. And at one stroke, by a most subtle mingling of firmness, moral pressure, and tenderness, Gabriel is to beckon him toward possible salvation.

We depart from the Cartagena harbor at 8:00 A.M. for the Fort of Terra Bomba, the two stars accompanied by a minor luminary, who at such times might be thought to shed a scant light on things.

Something becomes painfully apparent about Robert Bolt's

text as it touches on this scene. Here his strength overreaches itself. He demands all manner of convolutions to fill in the emotional spaces between words, so syncopated is the text. The two actors must attune their spirits to a stipulated dance, from damnation and despair, through awakening hope, and then come what may. But the challenge is not matched by Bolt's text; the dance is so choreographed as to demand impossible leaps against all laws, whether of gravity or grace. Or so it seems to me and, as things develop, to the actors and director as well.

In one form or another, Jeremy and Robert must answer such questions as: does the Jesuit have a sense of scoring merit here, as he wrestles for the sanity and soul of Mendoza? Is he invoking formulas of airy forgiveness as a cover for his own human emptiness? And again, does there exist in Father Gabriel, a sense that he is not not altogether unlike the remorseful killer languishing before him? And if such a sense is alien to him, is not the Jesuit indictable for a form of pharisaism? Also, does he feel depleted, or exhilarated, by this encounter of wits and hearts, this wrestling match between the demonic and the Holy Spirit? Is he crowing inwardly at scoring points, or is there a sense of being the lowly instrument of grace and truth?

We discussed in this regard another friendship, that of Ignatius and Francis Xavier—a theme that was central to the beginnings of the Order. I told the long, drawn out process of yin and yang, as Ignatius fought to turn this splendid worldling toward weighty matters of the spirit and how Xavier wavered and feinted, the spirits tumbling him about. Ignatius saw his volatile friend not as another "soul to be won," but as a brother whose talents complemented his own, "the very half of his soul." Ignatius saw him as someone of promise and achievement, someone who would be indispensable to his enterprise.

I thought of that "wise blood" Flannery O'Connor writes of. The wisdom of Ignatius in regard to Xavier and other potential members of the Company; those of promise or renown in the world would be most apt for the work of God.

Raising the foregoing questions may perhaps complicate the already difficult scene, but I believe they can only enrich it. Gabriel has in mind (or does he?) that this beaten and broken figure will rise again, to other works than those of blood. And Mendoza, pitiable, ignorant as the unborn or the newly dead, will one day be flooded with such stern resolve as to set him on unforeseen roads. Mendoza will rise from the dead.

Last night, in view of today's difficult filming, I introduced the possibility of a fast to Jeremy. He was attracted to the idea as a therapeutic, in view of decisions and insights of some import. So the two of us will undertake a gaunt diet for the day.

I'm sitting here quietly in a room of the Fort. The scene is a "ward in the hospital for incurables." Beds are spread with tattered sheets, ghastly mosquito netting is draped about. Joffé, De Niro, and Irons have been cloistered for some two and a half hours; no filming as yet.

In the course of the day, Jeremy and I talked much of Merton. I recalled the story of his Columbia days, a life on the wild side, but one slowed little by little to a human pace. I recalled an episode I so love, how he brought roses in midwinter to an ill mother in a walk-up flat in Harlem. In all her life, the only relief she had known were bland staples, the canned goods and potatoes offered by the unimaginative. But Merton brought roses, and she wept like a child.

The episode touched on a quality of relief that must mark the actor's attitude. There is nothing more deadly unbearable than a "religious message" without humor or verve.

They made five takes of long shots of the inert bundle on the pallet, with Jeremy hovering above like a hound of heaven. Jeremy afterward, "Did you believe the scene?" Roland joined us, "Yes, that's the minimum, that we're believable." And then I, "No, not the minimum. For me, that says everything—aura, bodily gesture, conviction, coherence, simplicity."

The pivot of the film: the two meet in a contest between grace and damnation and neither knows the outcome. Everything in the film leads to this center and radiates from it. The hoopla and extravaganza are thereby placed where they belong, displaced from center eye. A new center is created; within its burning glass is the exorcising of loneliness, remorse, and despair by an overwhelming and merciful courage . . .

Off the set and on to life! My entrepreneur leaned over massively at the dinner table, his big seegar all but making an impromptu ashtray of my ear. "As of the weekend," he rasped, "Two thousand pounds of rice and two thousand pesos were delivered to the nuns in the barrio." Thus spoke the biggest heart since Moses.

Terra Bomba. The extras lounge about in the devastating sun and here and there in the scant shade sit nuns, patients, soldiers, remnants of the lost ark of time. A few soldiers sleep along the cannon barrels, others stretch out on sacks of grain, looking for all the world like casualties after battle. Now toward 5:00 P.M., Jeremy and Robert are still within the hospital ward, sweating out "that scene"; close-ups now, I'm told, and no end in sight. A long, long travail for all concerned. Those of us outside waited as though we were expecting word from a delivery room—or a deathbed.

The moon is up, but the sun torches the earth; and as though respectful of that vast swath of flame, the moon abides in the wings, a ghostly presence keeping its distance.

Another scene is run on the parade ground of the Fort. A priest intones a Latin blessing on troops before battle. They shout out a basso profundo "Amen." They would of course have understood nothing of the words; and the commander who signals the amen and the priest who prays are likewise automatons. Church and state have arranged the scene and its consequence to their mutual benefit. No wonder the poor soldiers, who in life would shortly kill or be killed, obey with gusto, like Milton's "silly sheep."

I wonder why I am so little concerned about this "Jesuit thing" which so engages my British fellow Jesuit? Our Order, as he urges upon every comer, must be portrayed accurately ad unguem . . . In contrast, I keep battling from day to day to understand the human substance of whatever scene, glad that there are others with more sensitive noses for nice points, jots, and tittles.

On the other hand, it seems to me that if the film is not to be a waste, deeper questions have to be posed. Let the questions resist all answers, if they will; let them hang in the air if they so choose. They will nonetheless shed a measure of light on the proceedings.

For example, what qualities in the missioners met and won the hearts of the Indians?

What mingling of truthfulness and sound tactic worked the human wonder of the *reducciónes*—the unlettered native artisans and the schoolmen of Europe together creating a community of justice, dignity, and peace?

And what images and rhythms convey the impalpables of faith, moral coherence, and cultural adaptiveness?

And perhaps most important of all, how did the missioners confront death and the destruction of their dream? How did they confront their own death, coming toward them relentlessly (in loneliness, privation, the long march) and then arriving in total catastrophe?

Raising such questions might help us create images that blaze with truthfulness and consequential beauty. But I would as soon labor to teach an ape to don pantaloons, as waste my time instructing someone as to "how one acts like a Jesuit."

Thursday, May 2. We're to be decked out today for the stormy and sumptuous scene in the courtyard: a general assembly of Jesuits, settlers, the papal delegate and his entourage, the setting for the verbal battle between Mendoza and Altimirano. The scene has been tricky from the start, as the Jesuits emerge from Bolt's text somewhat like disaffected adolescents. And the provincial, for all the world like a tyrannical schoolmaster out of Dickens, is instructed to "hiss" at the assembled clerics at one point, "Silence!" All a bit much.

Today two good hours with Bob De Niro. Waiting for this to happen was another instance of my own impatience, faced with time and its delays and vagaries. He began by explaining the events at the Fort during the difficult filming with Jeremy. (I had been first instructed by Roland to be present for the scene, then was disinvited.) Bob explained in a way I found disarming that he can never bear to be "observed" during a take, that he must work at things without a third party present, that the truth of the scene must come only from himself.

This was fine; the episode was closed. We proceeded to discuss the *Spiritual Exercises* in some detail, the Jesuit formation Mendoza would be thought to undergo, the course of studies, priesthood, the third year of novitiate. I have a sense that the ice has broken, and he and I are drinking for the first time from the same stream.

Moods tend among us to a positively symphonic variation, high-C strings to tubas. Much depends on the degree of isolation, on whether a given scene has sent up fireworks or merely crash-landed, or on the momentary clash or melding of egos. What a blessing are a few books in the wilds, and the appetite so assuaged!

I thrive like a pig in a blanket. Most of the time.

Friday, May 3. I set down these fragments in the comparative quiet of the courtyard of Santo Domingo. In the church, they've concealed the altar, a nineteenth-century horror, behind a reredos of great restraint and splendor, in the style of the mission. Magnificent!

Last night, supper with our British Jesuit. I must record admirable restraint on my part, as with bottomless volubility he enlarges on the failure of the filmmakers to conform to something (he calls) Jesuit style and discipline. I'm invariably sunken in confusion, at a loss during such monologues, not being at all certain or (to tell the truth) terribly interested in his insular version of eighteenth-century mission life and practice.

Granted, the film takes considerable license with certain facts. Where he and I part company is on the subject of allowable limits. For example, the film introduces a Guarani Indian as a Jesuit placed in charge of a considerable mission. Now, no

Guarani, we are told on reputable authority, was received in the Order for the hundred-and-fifty-year span of the missions. This is a plain matter of fact. And the film contradicts it, to say the least. And Father rants interminably.

What to think? I tend to look on the episode as a species of sign of a better and different future now present and accounted for, for it is also a fact that in our century, all sorts and hues of "indigenous people" have been received in the Order and are presently exercising considerable authority in our midst.

I must also report that I detect in the quotes from the original missioners a whiff of arrogance, even of contempt for the Indians, once the subject of "intelligence" is raised. What the padres extolled (in themselves) and mourned the absence of in the Indians was evidently their (extremely limited) cultural understanding of the term, European, abstract and scholastic.

But what, one is inclined to inquire, is one to make of the extraordinary musical and artistic talents of the Indians? And might it not be further argued that an intemperate judgment on them and their capacities actually inhibited further possibilities, indeed implied that an arbitrary norm had been planted in mission ground, a wall, a boundary? "Them" and "us," and never the twain shall be one.

One has seen this sort of preemption before. In the case of candidates and younger members of the Order. Early decisions are made as to what a Jesuit is capable of, decisions that peg him to earth for a lifetime. To describe the ruin that ensues one would have to assemble images from a theater of cruelty or absurdity, or from Beckett—someone stuck up to his neck in (rapidly or slowly) hardening cement.

My British opposite number ("opposite" is in this case highly apposite) keeps shooting messages off to Roland; I even encourage him, judging that his letters help blow off sulphurous

steam. But his postulates with regard to the film would raise
hair on a bocci ball. For example, "It is not made apparent in
the film that every Jesuit, on whatever trek, carries with him a
Mass kit and a breviary." And again, "It should be made clear
that any Jesuit in formation is in constant contact with a
spiritual director and confessor."

Now such disciplines must be counted laudable (and I confess often to being lax in their regard). The Mass kit business
is something else again—balderdash. For the rest, one is perhaps justified in inquiring how strongly these religious forms
bear upon one's attitudes toward others. My friend of the Mass
kit, for example, makes no secret of his approval of capital
punishment, war, military service, and Ms. Thatcher's treatment of the poor of Britain. He airs such attitudes publicly, with
a kind of lethal innocence. Indeed his view of the world seems
marmoreally installed, not to be softened, let alone swept away,
by copious infusions of heavenly dew—such as are offered by
Jesuit rules, Mass kits, or even by the gospel.

As the French say, it makes to wonder. Is the discipline a
self-justifying "system," a summoning of "the law that jus-
tifies"—an abomination energetically denounced by Paul's
Letter to the Christians of Rome?

The faces of the "young Jesuit" extras strike me as quite
unprepossessing. I can't help contrasting these streetwise, distracted exemplars with the serenity and recollected sanity of
our novices at home.

And yesterday, horrors! Two of the becassocked urchins
broke out in fisticuffs at the tea table! It was a skirmish over a
sweet bun, which went flying through the air. The two were
separated with some difficulty, and the work rolled on.

* * *

We're mucking through the second day of filming in the courtyard. Swathed in sweaty Jesuit cassocks, we feel like Darwinian specimens marooned somewhere between sea and land, neither swimmers nor ambulators.

Betimes I solace myself with snatches from Raissa Maritain's *Adventures in Grace.* I find her, years after a first reading, almost unbearably ethereal. No doubt, I reflect with a pang, she and Jacques were drawing upon resources long since aborted or exhausted. One wonders indeed what they would make of the present pope—or for that matter of the current French church . . .

Last night we were urged to assemble—everyone, even those remotely connected with the film—for what was referred to in fun as our "graduation photo." De Niro changed from his cassock into his dashing hidalgo costume, the old, worldly guise of his preconversion.

I'm tempted to think, in my worse moments, that a kind of veneer is being laid on for the occasion by the actors. When required, the surface can assume a "religious" look; just as on other occasions, it creates for the duration, a philanderer, a parent, a healer, and so on. I submit this only in passing, as the fruit of considerable inexperience. But still . . .

Sunday, May 5. We're here one month today, and it's a workday to boot. It's also, I'm told consolingly, our last day in the sweatbox. The costume designers and fitters, Italians who outfit us each morning with unexampled good humor, are the true heroes of the operation. They commonly start at 4:00 A.M. and often work until after 7:00 P.M. . . . Huzzah and thank you!

*   *   *

A few of us were invited at the end of the day to a palatial residence in the old city for a drink and converse. We entered directly from the street, majestic court opening upon court, and at the last interior space, a swimming pool! All very easy on eye and spirit. But after having slogged through the barrio only a mile distant from this urban Eden, I was afflicted with a strange sense of being abducted and held somewhere, in a place utterly bizarre, unfamiliar, faintly ominous, especially when I was told of further emoluments—a yacht and a splendid horse farm near Bogotá . . .

One actor said feelingly, "People don't realize what goes into the making of a film. I've had fifty years in the theater, totally engrossing, constantly on my toes. But yesterday I sat on a damn dais for twelve hours in that infernal getup [deep purple ecclesiastical camp] repeating over and over like a circus ape two words: 'Continue, Father!' . . . "

Overheard at table. Actor 1, highly surcharged with philosophic opinionations: "I think we're here in the world only on behalf of nature, for procreation!" Actor 2, seldom heard from: "Then we're to measure the length of our civilization by the length of your prick?" End of exchange.

Throughout the long, steamy day, Jeremy kept his cool. Nothing daunted him: place, time, weather, repetition, heat, cigarettes, meager sleep. It was sheer disciplined British tour de force. Again and again, for a matter of hours in the tropical sun, he walked two hundred feet from the Cardinal to the Indian child. His very pace was a form of poetry, he walked like a liquefied leopard. He touched the child and returned to confront Altimirano with the words, "These, our people, are fleeing—from slavery."

So I record my admiration for actors' discipline, their endurance and good temper. Even to a degree, I celebrate their ego, that delicate honeycomb of stone, a veritable Great Reef; over it the tides of fortune wash and wash. And all in vain.

Note of Absolutely No Moment. De Niro has two armed guards keeping twenty-four-hour watch outside his hotel room, on the set, everywhere he ventures. This arrangement, I am told, is ordered by the insurance moguls; there is fear the star might be abducted and held for a royal ransom, say, the twenty-million-dollar budget of the film.

I am summoned at 4:00 P.M. to consult with Jeremy, Bob, and Roland. The famous apology scene is our subject. (In the film, Gabriel orders Mendoza so to respond, consequent on his public outburst before the Cardinal.) There are enough ambiguities here to choke a Solomon.

Let me try not to choke. Gabriel is agitated in spirit not because Mendoza lied (he did not), but because his shouting match was imprudent to a ruinous degree. He told the truth—slavery is the common practice in the territories of both Spaniards and Portuguese. But the truth, so told, has put a lethal weapon in the hands of the opposition, determined as they are to destroy the mission. What better incentive indeed than the excuse that a Jesuit (albeit so lowly and recent a novice as Mendoza) should have publicly insulted their rotten eminences? Draconian measures are sure to follow, an ironic case of virtue reaping its reward.

How to put all this together—folly, virtue, courage, intemperance, consequence?

I ventured that the criminal trial of nine of us in King of Prussia in 1981 might offer some light. On the witness stand I put my "crime" this way: "I could not not do this."

In the case of Mendoza, a vow of obedience must hold two realities in uneasy suspension, an all but intractable dilemma: on the one hand, the common good (the human rights of Indians, an exalted good indeed), on the other, the citadel of conscience, which the church has repeatedly vindicated, at least in principle.

There is simply no describing the corrupt, sinuous world-weariness summoned up by Ron, our Portuguese slave trader. Nor, for that matter, the arrogant imperialism of the Cardinal. Nor indeed, the impeccable style of Father Gabriel, as hour after clammy hour, Jeremy plays the soul of this priest—his dignity, mild strength, lucidity.

It may be thought that evil is a stereotype—except for that evil that is cursed by greatness. But Jeremy is no cliché. He blazes, hue after hue, as a common fire might, when a handful of precious spice is thrown in it.

Livy: ". . . a people who think life not worth living, unless they bear arms. . . . They prefer death to peace, while others prefer death to war." The types are portrayed in the film—the slave-trading Spaniard and Portuguese, Mendoza prior to conversion.

A type of whom Livy is ignorant (or ignores) is our Cardinal, whose robes and status grant him a meticulous distancing from violence. And yet there's no distance after all, or not much. His weapons are different, that is all—duplicity, the weighing of "lesser evils," ego, the feints of power politics.

*   *   *

Conversation in the barrio.

A North American (fervently, a veritable Improvement Manager at Large): "But surely there are all sorts of jobs to be had here. The sewers want digging, decent homes want building, markets could be opened, the people might bake their own bread . . . endless, really, possibilities!"

Priest (with the dead calm of One Who Lives amid It All): "Our people won't work at anything they don't enjoy."

Well, well, talk about the clash of cultures. Granted, the "enjoyment" is somewhat hard to grasp, existing as it does amid inhuman or subhuman conditions. On the other hand, one thinks of the incapacity of millions of people elsewhere (rich and poor alike, in England, America, and other places) to enjoy literally anything in life—whether jobs, affluence, good homes, satiety—and a light is cast on the remark of the barrio priest, and more on the genius of the Fathers of the mission.

Which is to say, they made labor enjoyable and enjoyment profitable. The abounding capacities of the Indians—for music, art, architecture, carving—these were woven in a dance celebrating an enhanced and vindicated humanity. As the Fathers came to realize this one by one, eventually all of them joined the dance. They were learners too, and perhaps being Jesuits, they danced in spite of themselves.

The enterprise had sprung from a sound basis, the right finger on the right stop of the flute, so to speak.

Long to-do in the afternoon concerning scenes to be done with Jeremy, Bob, and my fellow Jesuit. With the latter and myself, things used to start badly and worsen. Now things start badly and stay there—an improvement of note in an imperfect world.

*   *   *

The news reaches us at evening; it is indeed ominous. Roland collapsed on the set—exhaustion, dehydration. He is taken to the naval hospital and ordered to rest for an unspecified time. We lose at least two days of filming. No big deal—the main issue is Roland's well-being.

With regard to one character in our entourage: one left foot in his mouth, the other tapping a worn-out tune.

Or again: to be so certain, and so wrong! To be so wrong, because so certain!

And yet again: the cat swallows the canary, digests the feathers, and spits up the meat. And this is called living.

A witty letter arrives from Helen Woodson, mother of seven disabled children, who was guilty of a nonviolent action against nuclear war and was just sentenced to eighteen years in prison. How courageously she sets her face to the hideous future that boxes her in! On my part, admiration beyond words.

And I think, could I not for the moment substitute admiration of God for adoration, and all to the good? "I am in awe, made thoughtful by your great deeds. But I am in no wise diminished or put to naught, because You are You, and I a lesser being . . ."

It has an echo of the psalms; I'm in good company.

Thursday, May 9. A remarkable sound on awakening, the gentle hiss of rain, the first relief in five months in this parched mouth of creation.

Then at breakfast Jeremy and wife Sinead appeared with champagne and kisses. And I knew a different birthday than envisioned had dawned.

The shadow is sixty-four years long.
Ungainly it shambles on before
muttering distempered to itself,
Grow old! grow old!

Dawn is up, the man walks
in dawn, behind the smear of shadow,
disowning it. "Darkness
cast by me, I cast far from me,"
he sings to himself. His soul
he holds like a burning glass before.
And like a soul in him burns
the concentrate of dawn.

Nevertheless, duty must prevail. We repaired once more to Santo Domingo to attempt the wild and wooly scene between an adversary and De Niro. It bumbled and stumbled along for two hours, attempting some four or five minutes of credible exchange.

A stratospheric atmosphere prevailed, barely breathable, induced by those to whom the better is at times the enemy of the good.

Such is of course an impossible luxury in the great world, due to pangs of hunger and the landlord at the door. But here, since money is no object, we can fool and falter about almost at will. The condition could induce depression, but I twitch my suspenders with a twang and summon a different mood.

A wondrous birthday supper on the town redeems the day—Ron and the Ironses and gifts and much palaver and joking, all despite Jeremy's wretched back pains.

Friday, May 10. We're at work, Jeremy is wan with his wrenched back, and Roland looks somewhat like Lazarus just before the divine summons. And still we plug along.

Consumption was seldom more conspicuous. We've passed seven hours trying to achieve a four-minute sequence, the apology of Mendoza before the Cardinal. I suppose (sigh) everyone undergoes such a day, but rarely, or self-inflicted mayhem would become a commonplace.

Sometimes the sun rises in the evening. We worked on the set until 7:00 P.M. Then a call came, a meeting in Roland's room concerning tomorrow's text and scenes. As our discussion went on, David Putnam sat a little apart, on the floor, descanting on the financial realities of our film. In sum, we were spending too much day by day to be able to linger indefinitely on Circe's Isle munching lotus, all the while, so to speak, the devil taking the hindmost hog.

So be it. That chastening homily completed, Jeremy arranged late supper with De Niro, Brother Lawn, and myself. This went more or less beatifically, until 11:30. Quite a twenty-four hours, all in all!

Saturday, May 11. Roland continues patient, determined to give the stars prime time. We're three days behind schedule, and the production moguls wear a haunted look, as though at the sound of millions of pesos falling into the void.

Strange, but I suppose predictable, how under such intense days and nights, some friendships move closer, others prove mere shelters from gusty weather.

The film cannot be thought of, much less undertaken, apart from the thorough soul testing of all concerned. Which is to say, we have on our hands quite a hot property, to lend the inelegant phrase a new twist, hot that is, and therefore dangerous, apt to burn one. Which is not to assert that we will measure up to its moral and esthetic demands.

* * *

Sunday, May 12. After the honeymoon, one settles, even in paradise, into a fairly predictable rhythm: one day humdrum, the next vexatious, the third incendiary, and so on. Two of our company are like Blake's tigers, burning bright with (too much) fearful symmetry. Another is a daytime haunt and a nightly grin, as of a vanishing Cheshire cat reversed in time.

Evening. By chance in the local crèperie I encounter David Putnam. Among other topics, he told of seeing the "rushes" today and how superbly Jeremy came through. No surprise here. We also talked at length of how much more difficult De Niro's role is.

Ten of us on a free day drove north of the city, then launched into dugout canoes at a fishing village. We were poled and rowed through a system of canals and mangrove clumps. Many splendid white herons, but nary an alligator.

Ian, the young British tutor, Jeremy, and I walked most of the way back under a glaring carmine sunset that shook the world, first to embers, then to ash. Jeremy climbed about with his camera—the local kids had great fun at this—but he was finally waved off angrily by the father of one.

Hard to predict—some love to pose and preen, others remind me of the fisherfolk of Senegal or the towering herdsmen of Kenya, who feel that to take a photo is to steal, literally, something of the spirit. I understand this, being so often victimized myself.

Wednesday, May 15. The morning starts inauspiciously with the usual wardrobe ceremony; I am draped in the damp woolen cassock, which in an hour or two will be wringing wet.

Nightlong, the dream machine has been tumbling me about

like a ping-pong ball. How afflicting these dreams can be, when either remembered or anticipated. They offer a bleak landscape, usually around themes of prison—those I love, myself, or all of us in lockup by someone's irrational whim.

Our hair is trimmed by the skilled makeup crew. They have fastened photos of us on the barbers' mirrors; no detail shall escape likeness to the phiz and pate of some weeks ago. We are ministered to by the makeup women; their hands are gentle as white mice.

I also view a wig of human hair, assembled strand by strand, to be donned by my semblable, the stunt man who is to dare the cliffs and falls of Argentina in my place, for which I am grateful it goes without saying.

We arrived in the courtyard. I am greeted by the Jesuit pastor of San Pedro; warm felicitations are exchanged with the help of a translator. It appears that my notoriety has preceded me. The Jesuits are appraised of my pilgrim's progress—Vietnam, prison, and so on. Heartening indeed.

Current reading, thanks to a bit of forethought in carrying a bundle of books along to Colombia: Joyce, *Portrait of the Artist*; Stringfellow, *Politics of Spirituality*; Wendell Berry, *Agriculture and Civilization*; Pascal, *Pensées*; Kierkegaard, *Attack on Christendom*. (The latter two are great complainers and not to be taken for a steady diet; they turn a liver to jaundice and dim the native wit.) Night reading: Wilkie Collins; *The Moonstone*.

One of our young English actors grows restive. The days are burdensome; he tolerates them in desultory fashion. It galls him, he says, to hang about with so little to do. I nod to his mood, understanding to a degree the affliction of ennui in someone who has no taste for study or reading. Paradise à la Hilton? Alas, the worm of boredom dieth not.

The cry of "Action! Roll it!" goes on and on, a very trump of judgment. The cameras consume everything in view, after an ideal world has been created and set in place, down to the last curl of hair and the least fold of a garment.

Such meticulosity, such a passion for perfection of a rather restricted kind! At the same time, the elaboration of detail risks confounding trees, twigs, the fall of light and shadow, with the great forest. But if the film is not to fall of its own top-heavy splendors, it must contain a counterweight (or better, weightlessness) so that it soars aloft like a winged throne. Soul must shine through.

Friday, May 17. Many have transported here great mounds of baggage that would set the concupiscent eye agleam. The follies of excess appear all the more glaring in the pitiless light of Latin poverty. Why do we need so much? Pitiful stabs at immortality?

"The love of possessions is a disease with them" (American Indians).

Last night we celebrated the end of the first Cartagena phase. A gala, a very spree. The lawn of the hotel was arranged to welcome some three hundred. The tables were set like spokes around the circular lily pool. A dance floor floated in the midst, and an orchestra made hokey and honky-tonk by turns.

And what a transmogrification under the moon, as the workhorses of day became the tropical aviary of night! The Italian costumers were their very own triumph; the hairdressers favored us with curls, crowns, hirsute superstructures of superb daring. The actors shone on everyone benignly. We were hundreds of weavers and workers of fantasy, and for a few hours were living the fantasies we created.

All that is, except for De Niro and I, whose costumes for work or play are an indistinguishable dun, a kind of protective noncoloration. I sat with him and his lady and Putnam. Everyone moved to and fro dancing, except Bob and I, two old numbers hiding out from fate. We sat there, enjoying it all, he with his unlit stogy and each of us with a wineglass.

Saturday, May 18. By Avianca to Santa Marta.

TO SAINT PETER CLAVER
(*on leaving Cartagena, 1985*)

The noble dead lie in unmarked graves
    countless in my generation,
known only to God, who moulds faces
with potter's thumb, wheel, and treadle,
then, holds the broken dead like a lover
    weeping for the wrecked work.

Harmless, pretentious as puff pigeons
the generals, their war-horses, their public faces
prance in midair, going
nowhere. Their war cries pollute public places.

    A town at war, soldiers
    led to slaughter
    march through public places
    baa-baaing like sheep.
    Preternatural their tears
    their noble mockery and mime.
Known only to God, they fall in Unknown places.

At San Pedro Claver, the saint reposes
"Slave of the slaves," his self-entitlement and glory
a lamp of apocalypse in the bridegroom's hand.
Outside, beggars, cripples hover
apocalyptic spirits of earth and air,
purgatorial bodies and souls
(could we but read not run, like blinded sheep baa-baaing!)

In the public place, a general, his war-horse,
    fused gargoyles, pour their mad
molten rhetoric, mad trumpets blare
    on the innocent air.

The saint turns to rest, an unextinguished lamp, his tongue
foresworn to silence before mad Pilate,
    the absurd stick sword,
the bronze bluff of imperium melting like wax or flesh.

Silence, innocence, soul, sweet revenge
of truth outraged.
    O might the slaughter-bound sheep
    flock to this well of life,
    draw from the throat of the dead
    than "baa-baa, pity the death-bound
    sheep in sheep's clothing!"—
    a mightier work and word!

Pray; sheep cast off their fleece,
mutton and muddle. The general
pluck from his breast the brassy clock
    tick-tocking doom on doom,
      cast it in the blaze
the saint in his combustible body lit,
a watchman's fire on Cartagena's walls.

Conversation en route with Puttnam. Still much puzzlement over the ending of the film. There is some sentiment for

retaining the scene as Bolt has envisioned it: Father Gabriel at prayer with his people in the mission church, all of them perishing there.

I maintain that this is unsatisfactory from every point of view. It reduces Father Gabriel and his people to passive victims; he is seen as someone unable to imagine a gesture of faith and political consequence.

Much remains to be sweated over, as we try to come up with an image of hope and risk, all in favor of liberation—of both Jeremy and his people.

Outside Santa Marta, we're lodged in a beautiful hotel just completed; we're in fact the first guests. A main building of great charm in the Spanish manner, an open airy court giving on a kind of village of cabinos and a pool, and the sea beyond.

The idea, as I understand it, is to have the actors all together in one nest. We are to be mutually improving, to shed a healing balm on one another's ego when required. So goes the theory, enlightened or not. Actually, it presupposes a degree of forebearance and discipline I'm not at all sure we're equal to, but relentless time and solitude will tell.

Here by the open sea, there is nothing of the inspired tackiness that enlivened the *via purgativa* of Cartagena. No raunchy little bars and hideaways within reach of a consumptive taxi. Nature in full cry, in excess; sea and sky, a blistering bonanza of creation. And then, of course, one another.

Ian and I took a long jaunt by the sea and came on a bizarre and disturbing episode. A group of fishermen offshore were lighting fuses and casting sticks of dynamite into the sea. It was a desperate last-ditch measure of the poor, seeking food. But

they do much harm to the coral reef and also destroy the beds
of fish, since the explosives kill everything within range. It was
a violent and dangerous method to boot, since we noted one or
another fisherman with mutilated hands.

A continuing perplexed discussion on the ending of the film.
Are we to concede, as in the theology of Milton, that evil had
best be granted the last word, that the evildoer is essentially
more interesting than the virtuous?

We are trying to imagine a better fate for Father Gabriel
(which is to imply we try to imagine something better by way
of life and life's ending for ourselves).

Puttnam said in his usual incisive way that Gabriel falters
or walks as steady as we do; and if we come on the truth of him,
we do great service for ourselves. He also wants Jeremy out of
the discussion, the theory being that his task is to act the scene,
once it is firmed up, something I don't by any means agree with.

By tomorrow, equipment will be set up at Gabriel's mission
in the jungle some fifty kilometers from the hotel. We'll be
transported to and fro in a fleet or more or less able (or disabled)
taxis.

Word reaches us of a recently discovered "lost city" compa-
rable to Machu Picchu of Peru. An invitation accompanies the
news, from the Colombian ministry of tourism, to visit the
wonder by helicopter.

One has a restive sense that under the thinnest of crusts,
Colombia is boiling with violence. Today there are armed
guards at the gates of our paradisiacal hostel. And this morn-

ing, a free day, as a convoy of actors and workers made for
Santa Rosa, they were stopped for unknown reasons by army
personnel and evicted from the cars.

We had our first Eucharist together, Jeremy and Sinead,
Ian, De Niro, and the other actors; Liam, Hines, and McAn-
nally. There was great palaver from most, as might be expected;
De Niro and Irons were musingly silent. We prayed for folk at
home, here and in Europe, for those in prison, for the poor and
victimized around us, for the women of Greenham Common—
also and with notable fervor for our own continued safety on
the mad roads of Colombia, which we perforce cast our lives
upon each morning.

We drove for the first time the careening kilometers to the
jungle. The splendid mission set is finished, all adobe and palm
leaves, modest, serviceable; at sight of it, one senses no violation
of the awesome wildness around. The birds scream and call
aloud to one another; the sun beats the earth like a fervent
drummer.

We left the autos by the river bank and proceeded for the
final mile in motor dugouts, leaping ashore like knowledgeable
primates on home turf. Shortly thereafter, the generators were
coughing and chugging away, and, best of all, the urns of coffee
arrived. Civilization laid claim to its outpost.

A flash flood has destroyed our footbridge; today the Don
Diego River wears an ominous look, far different from the
halcyon days when we waded and thrashed about happily, knee
deep in gentle water, hunting iguanas.

In our midst, even in the jungle, Colombian soldiers stalk
about in camouflage, bearing Sten guns. One of them patrols in

the wet sand not six feet from my writing stool. I remain unreassured.

One hardly dares lay aside so simple and ordinarily inedible an object as a pencil or pen; an unidentified flying faunum lands like a flash.

Twelve noon in the jungle; mad dogs and moviemakers are out in the noonday sun. Filming all morning, great industry and urgency apparent. I was set in the midst of a bevy of Indian children. One, afflicted with polio, hops about on all fours, in no way impeded or put down. Another little one is blind.

It was mandated from on high that we five Jesuits were to choose a sixth from among the extras to work henceforth with us. We interviewed a Spaniard, rather too smooth talking, and then a tall Swiss lad, Rolf, of late arrived in Santa Marta from a remote Indian village in the mountains. He had lived there in the wilderness for a year, raising corn and felling trees. He was our unanimous choice and, as events transpired, it was a sound one.

Patricia, the "continuity" expert, made one of her trenchant observations, quite in passing, as is her wont. During the morning's filming, she declared that I, surrounded as I was by the Indian children, appeared as "happy as a pig in shit." Well, well.

The fleas and mosquitos are an eighth plague, indescribably tenacious, a cloud of mini-demons. They hover and dart about, forever seeking an opening. They also render our wooly costumes doubly penitential, the fleas especially, addicted as they are to tender human parts such as the eyeball. And when the sun clouds over, invariably around noon, they issue forth seeking to devour.

The workmen make sport of the clerics, real or simulated. They salute me with malicious good humor: "Ciao, Padre . . . will you hear my confession?"

A weather warning is issued in midafternoon: everyone into the boats, the water is rising, flash floods are expected, get out while you can . . .

Good conversation with Sinead and Jeremy at supper about how our filming could fatally decline into a kind of wide-screen National Geographic series: "Innocent Savages Brought to Your Coffee Table in Three Issues." How we, the Jesuits, must be vigilant against this parody, passing more time with each other in a spirit of affection and inwardness.

Monday, May 20. A day of fun and frolic. We set out, like the sunset of the empire, in a fleet of cars to view the national park and its beaches. We enter an enormous grove of coconut trees; slowly, the Caribbean thunders make themselves heard.

> The National Park gave on the sea
> that fought to a frenzied impasse.
> The land countered, set a warrior's shoulder
> so cut its losses.

> We entered; a crude lettered board:
> THIS LAND BELONGS TO THE COLOMBIAN PEOPLE
> SOME OF WHOM ARE DEAD
> SOME LIVING
> BUT MOST ARE UNBORN.

We trod warily
as though on All Souls' Night,
parting the vines
thick as warriors' wrists—

Borrowers, ancestors, heirs
in a land not ours.
The unborn, the dead
a cloud of witnesses
around, overhead.

Set within the sublime reserve, like a toad on a nest of gold, was the hacienda of a local hustler. We were invited to pass the day on his acres. The place, as someone remarked and everyone sensed, bore a malevolent mafia atmosphere. (Our host, a smooth-tongued number, is also the largely absentee manager of our hotel.) He was on this occasion at some pains to explain Colombian politics, to merely desultory interest on our part. He introduced an unprepossessing sidekick as a candidate for mayor of Santa Marta. Were this character to prevail, it seemed to us, the unlucky citizens were well advised to lock up their valuables.

The high (or low) point of the festivities approached. Our host waxed eloquent on his plans, as minister of tourism, for the "development" of the famed "lost city." He proposed, with that mad seriousness endemic to his kind, to "build a cable car of some forty kilometers to reach the site."

At that point, the eyes of my mind slammed closed like iron shutters. Here, in full panoply, effrontery and irresponsibility were at one. And the public be damned. And the lost city twice doomed.

*   *   *

Puttnam misses not a beat. When invited to join us on this ill-fated venture he said, "No, I'm afraid I'd punch that playboy in the teeth. He's supposed to do his job here, managing the hotel. He has no business neglecting us to organize fiestas." Indeed and a fervent amen!

Ominous news on our return. The floods have reached the Indian village; all families have had to be evacuated. They will be residing for several days at least in various hotels in Santa Marta. The village is to be rebuilt on higher ground. All single male Indians have agreed to stay behind and help.

Tuesday, May 21. On instructions from Roland, Jeremy and I are to spend a day with the Indians in town, sequestered as they are for the time being in three or four hotels.

The British medico takes a somber view of the flooding and its possible consequence. Sewage from the outdoor toilets has already escaped and spread about. "If we're lucky (and I don't expect we will be, given the past), we can only hope for another flood and recession to carry the stuff away."

Meantime, he makes fairly drastic recommendations. Three inches of the infected soil must be dozed off and buried elsewhere; fresh sand is to be spread over the area from the riverbanks. The new settlement must be placed on higher ground and the whole area carefully sprayed.

To lighten the fifty-mile run between the hotel and filming at the river, Jeremy plays a tape in the car, Handel's "Alleluia Chorus." I'm no great enthusiast of twenty trumpets blasting in my ears, but the music was offered by way of distraction from the perils of our hair-raising run and was so received.

The day was passed almost entirely in dugouts on the river.

I tend to a modest if not fearful view of such ventures: when
the solid earth is as unsteady as commonly appears, why walk
the waters? Heavily costumed as we are, it would indeed be
dangerous, were we to be upended.

3:00 P.M. These are quite possibly the first words in any
language to be penned in a tipsy Indian dugout some two feet
wide and twenty long. The fiction: in the bedraggled guise of a
weary Jesuit, I am voyaging toward home turf, the mission,
after at least a month on the jungle paths and portages. I voyage
in a brave fleet of ten canoes of this type; we form the escort
of the papal legate, Altimirano. He is deigning to visit the
mission, with a view to deciding our future, whether survival
or extinction. The latter, it is somberly believed by the Jesuits,
is far the more likely, though we keep our sorrowful premoni-
tions under our cinctures.

> On the Don Diego
> the dugouts assemble
> like a sublime children's charade:
> "By River, Indians and Jesuits Enter the Mission."
> In my hands
> a leather-bound volume:
> "Summa Theologica, Venice, 1773."
> I sit awash.
> The vast tome opens like the throat of a sage
> to "Article Eighty-four:
> Wherein Are Adduced Five Reasons
> Why God Is Named Love."
> (In quaint Latin) "Because God is source
> of love, because
> God creates for love, because
> God would have us love as we are loved,

because"—I raise my eyes,
the multifarious jungle leaves astir—
an open volume
grown voluble, uttering
reasons beyond number, for
love beyond reason.

The actors have just disembarked; we've enjoyed a fine box
lunch on a sandy spit. Some of us have stripped off our clammy
cerements and delight in a refreshing swim. The cassocks, dis-
carded gratefully, have steamed in the sun for an hour and are
all but dried. We don them again light-heartedly, ready for the
next three or four hours.

The Jesuit robes swath us, who shall be
like those originals, bones stacked and sacked
by vandalous time, sifted in God's great
hourglass upended. So we pass

as they did
into God's holy Son—
the Pardoner, his temporal flesh
vandalously, too, undone.

I touch the fabric; it rots. So time
touches me. I become
less bodily, like the sun
rising upon its light; more like the Son
as brother is belike. And heart
quickens its beat; entrance rite
into—believe it—being.

Thursday, May 23. We've undertaken the big climb toward
the falls. The mountain goes nearly straight up, like an arrow
slightly arced for more deadliness. I and the other Jesuits barely
hold on.

Earlier we were treated to the sight of a raving squad of renegade Indians (fiction upon fiction) led by their witch doctor decked out in a cloak of corn husks and a hideous mask. They bore aloft the body of a Jesuit played by a stunt man; the priest was fastened to a cross, barely living. They rushed along with their horrid burden and dumped it in the river.

"Cut scene!" And the crew rushed into the water to save our brave Bronco, who had landed dangerously, body down, and was floating downstream rapidly. Flipped over and brought carefully ashore, he appeared as unflappable as a platypus, apt for land or water . . .

This, according to the screenplay, is to be the opening scene of the film. One thinks it should have even jaded New Yorkers by the ears; but whether the heads will follow the hearing, and the heart the head, only God can tell.

In any case, we climbed and clutched the scant handholds, fell flat, held on for dear life. And all the while behind the little band of Jesuits, Mendoza followed like a shadow of something other than Providence (or was it Providence?) dragging his burden of guilt and redemption, straining and sweating against the impeding rope that much resembled a hangman's noose, that burden, for all the world like original sin embodied, balled up, snarled in its net, fastened to his body; his mad purpose, opaque to all others, was livid in his eyes.

The Jesuits, as the screenplay portrays them, have no part in his bizarre obsession; they neither undertook it nor advised it. But, in the person of the superior, Father Gabriel, they countenance it; Gabriel refuses to interfere or to allow any of them to interfere. Mendoza, as long as he purposes, as long as his wretchedness animates him, will drag through the jungle the weight of his sin: a clanking net filled with the mementos of his lurid glory, halbert, sword, helmet, leggings, breastplate.

The film is reticent; it makes no moral comment. It merely records, mercilessly, in images that stop the heart: Mendoza be damned or Mendoza be saved. The outcome can neither be manipulated nor foreclosed, as though we—actors, director, writer—in virtue of talent or insight or anything else were justified in playing God.

Whatever the outcome for this self-damned one, it will be surprising, and in that measure, as long as hope remains, a work of God.

And in allowing for the surprise, opening ourselves to it, refusing to interfere in these disciplines, which are matters of waiting and withholding and hearkening, in being faithful to these, we do our best to guarantee the integrity of the film. It is all very strange.

Mendoza, by atavism and instinct, keeps moving, keeps to a spoor, keeps within sight and sound of his (relatively) unimpeded friends. He struggles with fatalism and fierce gusto up that mountain of torment, that Calvary. The heat, the bugs, the burden—the Passion of Christ?

We had best go slow here; in metaphors, everything is not allowed. And it is a poor metaphor that is ignorant of its own poverty.

We climb; which is to say, we skitter and cling to roots and rocks and pass along ropes and water gourds and stretch out to one another a precarious handhold.

I forebear philosophies, as Hamlet advises, and keep my perplexities (almost) to myself. Almost. And here goes. Are these horrific images, succeeding one another pell-mell, apt for the enhancement of the spiritual understanding of the tribe? If not, to what end is all this technique and talent? And if so, alleluia indeed.

*   *   *

Saturday, May 25. Everyone remarks on the extraordinary dignity, self-possession, and good humor of the Indians. Someone volubly contrasted these qualities with "the cunning and sluggishness of the Colombian hands." What was never brought up was a comparison between the Indians and the Europeans, who, to be sure, love discussion, but dread like a plague being discussed.

In the canoes during the river scenes, one hears what is apparently a joke being passed along by the Indians, canoe to canoe; and a wave of spontaneous laughter rises, naturally as sunlight after shade. Pure delight!

And then, another scene. At the river landing at noon, a vast panoply of food appears. And a great hubbub ensues, as the Colombians rush to seize the first lunch boxes. (The Europeans, it goes without saying, had provided for themselves beforehand.) Our caterers raised a cry, "Indians first, Indians first!"

Meantime, taking in the scene with an exemplary silent contempt, the Indians stood there in attentive, charged awareness.

Sunday, May 26. Some fifteen of us were invited to supper at the De Niro cabino. Roland told a wonderful story. In the course of seeking a tribe of Indians who might take part in the film, he visited a number of villages. In one of these, he was told that a group of priests and nuns were celebrating the centenary of their missionary work in the area.

The chief of the tribe seized the occasion to question the priests. "What have you done for us in these hundred years?"

The priest: "We brought you the word of God."

The chief: "You did that not for us, but for yourselves. What else?"

"We translated the Bible in your language."

"This you did for your own honor. What else?"

"Our nuns work here in the dispensary. We've given you complete medical care."

Relentlessly, "This was also for your sake, not ours. And now we have a few more questions for you. Why are there no Indian doctors or lawyers after all your years among us? Why has no Indian become president of Colombia? Why, after your hundred years?

"Tomorrow our tribe gathers to mark your anniversary among us. And we are going to vote whether you are to remain or depart. If the vote goes against you, you will leave; one hundred years may well be enough."

The vote went five to one against the missioners, and off they went. And some years later, Roland concluded, there is an Indian doctor on the reservation, and other Indians are preparing for professional life.

The story sparked a great to-do about the film. The historical Jesuits decided, shortly after their arrival among the Guarani, that no Indian was capable of becoming a member of the Order. The decision was so enduring in fact, that it must be accounted a fiction in our film that a Guarani Indian is not only a Jesuit, but has been appointed superior of a mission. The conversation grew quite intense toward the end of the evening, turning on the missioners' closure of mind and their conclusion, arrived at so early on and evidently held to the end, that the Indians were "incapable of abstract thought," that they were apt only to imitate European artifacts, calligraphy, and architecture.

From day to day my doubts about being here, doing this work, grow less imperious. I am wondering about this. On the one hand, a nagging sense of doubt can be pernicious and enervating. On the other, to be clear of all doubt may mean that I grow callous, in virtue of the dolce vita so amply provided; I may be sliding into a kind of mordant tourism of heart, quite content to float with the jetsam.

Last night Roland was particularly eloquent on the subject of conversion. The topic came up naturally, as we move further into the film, especially into searching out the role of Mendoza. Roland used Saint Paul as his exemplar, the fall from horse on the road to Damascus. The explanation I thought excessively psychological but, coming from so good a man, nonetheless affecting.

If one explains Paul by the "breakup of personality in favor of a new integration," one is still saying nothing about the "light from heaven" or the voice "Saul, why do you persecute me?" These, as I would understand things, are abrupt signs of the onslaught of grace and by implication, a reproof to human preemption—including that of psychologists.

One perhaps may wonder too where this explanation, which I found so moving, leaves Roland? I would hesitate to think he has been seized by the light and is sitting the saddle all the more stubbornly. At the same time, I feel his explanation falls short of touching the heart of the Pauline scene.

Is psychology the opium of capitalists, as classism is the opium of Marxists?

We dwelt at length on the cultural difficulties implicit in the very words "mission" and "missionary." It seemed that an "age of faith," strong, coherent, and unified as it might be in the Europe of the seventeenth century, still had an obverse face, had great weaknesses built in.

Our century raises a far different question, even to raise it is painful beyond words. Do we "of the faith" have anything at all to offer, in the realm of truth, symbol, substance, hope in dark times, discipline—in sum, a viable tradition?

We have only the sorry strength of divided minds. So we insist on raising such questions as would lie inert, in abeyance, off to the side of the eye, so to speak, in "times of faith."

And yet, and yet. The questions we raise inch their way, worms that die not, toward the center of existence. They inhibit even as they claim and inhabit; they all but bring on a stalemate. Things fall apart; suppositions once held in common become fierce sources of contention. "Is there a God?" precludes the experience of God. Faith no longer occurs to us as a sublime benefitting of the human, favored by divine graciousness.

O those favored missioners, favored indeed, limited as they were by imperial arrangements. But how different the medium, how intense the message!

Up to our necks in the film as we are, we seldom ask what is going on here, under the routine and workaday. Nor do we seem equipped, for all our equipment, with the images and metaphors to lend sense to our work.

A few reflections, raised in no particular order, might help.

·Why do we delve into history to recreate a lost paradise, entering a foreign country and time, armed with sabers and old cannons, meantime employing "the natives" only as "extras" to the actors, who are themselves foreigners?

·Any realistic appraisal of our connection with the Indians and impoverished Colombians must be seen as that of master to slave, in a deadly economic sense.

·As for the Indians, we transport them (read, make foreigners of them) by immersing them in our fictions and techniques—

for what we are pleased to think of as a just wage—even while we remain ignorant of the consequences of their removal, consequences to their children and the future of the tribe. All this moreover while their survival even on their native ground remains precarious in the extreme.

·What are we after in all this? (What am I after?) I am gaining almost nothing, if I compare my sojourn here with last year's exposure to the realities of Central America. "A way of saying thank you to the Jesuits," as I put the project to superiors? But a thank-you must be more than an exercise in nostalgia or dependence, whether to the Order or to the past.

·We whiz along every morning from our hotel, past the barrios of Santa Marta, on our way to the filming. Those of the poor who can put their hands on a few pesos will undoubtedly, in a year or two, view our film, as will the middle class from New York to Tokyo. But to what end? To whose benefit?

·Are we merely adding weight to film history, piling image on image, film on film, Olympus on Etna—frivolity, ambition, rancor, gloss, laughter, violence, defeat, all to little avail, only in aid and abetting of our present plight and impasse—the exact ironic opposite of the purpose envisioned?

I have a sense that no doubts can tarnish: that our stars are men of integrity. At least in this limited sense they struggle and mull and reflect and study, all in order to give a human face to tragic events, a face capable of tears, nuances, purpose, and faithfulness. And more; in the present instance, they labor hard to convey such human drives and stalls and reverses, because they recognize the beauty of the lives of the missioners. This, their labor and self-giving, consoles me and calms my doubts.

Almost everyone associated with the film describes him- or herself to me as an "ex"—an ex-spouse, an ex-Catholic, and so on. Perhaps they do it out of deference to me, whom they commonly look on as an "ex-activist" (!). There is a nagging sense among them (and I insist in all sorts of ways on being a nag) that the world is going to hell in a hot-air balloon. But there is little thought given to the effort required to bring the basket safely down.

The blockage of imagination is at least in part along these lines: plethora of pesos, unlimited deluxe travel (invariably, so to speak, by hot-air balloon), multiple homes. The image industry offers a plausible world of security and well-being. The gas bag floats on, the gas flame blazes away, the world of misery and violence is viewed from above, from an esthetic, airy distance. Thus the illusions of a free-floating world and its rewards create illusion within.

I saw, propped against a shed a haunting and disturbing sight, a wax replica, its hands sheathed in plastic, of the "crucified Jesuit" whose demise forms the opening sequence of the film. The dummy is hung with a warning sign: "Careful. Fragile." The replica, and others like it of mercenaries and Indians, will be cast over the great falls in Argentina.

Here goes once more with second thoughts, all but crowding out the first. What is so terrifying a sequence meant to convey? Why does it open the film? (There is no recorded instance of such a method of martyrdom, though many Jesuits died violently in the missions.)

It strikes me that we have not honored for a long time the old Greek taboo against overt violence being portrayed onstage. Such events belonged "in the wings," merely to be reported or referred to or reflected on by the chorus. We have paid heavily for our madly literal effrontery, throwing images of blood and death about like a rampage in a slaughterhouse.

*   *   *

It's ironic and even laughable that I'm "in" the film somewhat in the way I'm "in" the church. Which is to say, in each
I have what is officially known as an "advisory role" or a "bit
part." The assignments conferred in each case are really unclas-
sifiable. In the church, since I'm ordained, I cannot quite be
reduced to an "extra." But on the other hand, I will never
qualify for a star role. And in the film, in some mysterious
monkish way, I am found useful—to render the actors, pro tem
and in a manner of speaking, pneumatic. A sort of air pump
operator, so to speak. Delightful!

Wednesday, May 29. "In the age of celebrity, the only truly
heroic act an artist can perform is to protect his vision and his
virtue by cloaking them in a modesty that is near to the secre-
tive" (Schickel). The statement, I think, is worth the whole
book *(Intimate Strangers)*, which in sum is not worth a great
deal.

The *reducciónes* (missions) had be destroyed because, in the
judgment of their enemies, the Jesuits had overreached themselves, had become, so to speak, too good for their own good.
The law of "balance in nature" (predator takes all) caught up
with them. Cloistered goodness could be borne with, but public
heroism was too much for that world (i.e., structures of cruelty
and cupidity) to bear.

A small number of the missioners were killed by a small
number of Indians who objected strenuously to the missioners'
objections to a quaint custom—namely, that defeated enemies
end up in the menu.

But the killing of the Jesuits was in a sense an act of pure
nature, the crime of a people who were, in most respects, infinitely superior to the European invaders of their continent;

generally the Indians stood apart from a "Christian" society of acquisitiveness, cruelty, and enslavement. The Indians were acting according to the old logic that decreed the death of the messenger, perhaps in this case, because he came bearing Good News.

But the main issue and cause of the destruction of the Jesuits lay elsewhere. The missioners, far flung as they were and deprived of access to the European course of events, did not understand what was gathering force; nor, with far less reason, did their Father General, or the court Jesuits and kings' confessors of Europe. Eventually, they joined forces to avert the catastrophe, but it was a case of too little too late. They all miscalculated the vitriolic fury of pure envy.

Europe, by no stretch of history or hope to be thought a kingdom of light, had sent the missioners forth. It blessed and honored them for a time; but the enterprise almost at once began to exceed the mandate. The missioners, it was agreed, were to extend the kingdom of God among the heathen. But they were by no means to interfere with the kingdom of this world, whose lucrative functioning required natives, whether heathen or converted, for slave labor. The Jesuits, to their honor, objected strenuously and consistently to this theory and practice of the "two kingdoms."

They insisted on making the natives into citizens of both realms, a dangerous undertaking on several counts. It vindicated the human rights of the newly converted and thus made them, "conscienticized" as they were, unfit for willing servitude. Simultaneously, the missions and their insistence on the dignity and humanity of the Indians inevitably placed the humanity of thousands of Europeans in question. Thus, in the minds of settlers, slave traders, adventurers, mercenaries, and even some churchmen, did insult succeed injury.

The injuries were felt far and wide, even touching to the quick their Catholic highnesses of several European countries.

Everything in the film must be both stupendous and meticulous. Thus between takes, the hairdressers rush in to adjust De Niro's hyacinthine hair, almost as though he were a corpse to be rearranged after a lengthy journey in a box. Thus also, each of hundreds of costumes must be thread perfect and pass the muster of a vigilant wardrobe manager, who can spot a flea on a waistcoat at a hundred yards!

Friday, May 31. The main actors are surpassing mere typecasting (impeccable priest; renegade turned Jesuit). The "type" is by every count a catastrophe, ricocheting off a "type" of audience or society. Two sides of a distorting mirror. "Any image is preferable to none."

The type is a pernicious opposite number to a saint. The first, a rush toward ego and celebrity, is a kind of revenge of the culture against the living, while the saint offers a model, a realized ideal that becomes, in death, indefinitely fecund. The type responds to the public appetite for alienation, ideology, and manipulation. The saint acts as a source to be emulated by a community of believers.

The elaborate game proceeds on the river. This time a battle scene, the bad guys losing to the good guys after a few sporadic shots with no more lethal content than children's firecrackers. What a wonderful war in which no one gets killed! And would that all strife could work itself out as harmlessly! Rubber-tipped arrows, smoke puffing from a smoke pot, a kind of ketchup carnage, workers and onlookers getting free rides and front seats in the dugouts. Much good humor as the take ends and tea arrives by boat. People laugh away like children out of school.

When the foolish is taken seriously, or when the seriousness of history is foolishly dealt with, we reach the breaking point of coherence and belief. A good film takes its chances. A bad one starts with good intentions perhaps, stretches things to the breaking point—and beyond. Then the believable dissolves in pretensions of various kinds.

Yesterday a hundred or so mercenaries, extras, tired of the many repeats of a single shot, at the end of the day one and all plunged overboard into river. Quite a splash! Whether they were stoned on grass, as reported, or merely decided on a bit of drama under their own aegis, the outcome was the same. Wigs were ruined beyond repair, costumes faded, ran, and shrank. And today, the same gents must don the same damp garments of yesterday's adventure.

The Indians, being nearly naked to start with, took their own cooling dip as a matter of course and without misadventure. Thus was Rousseau, in a manner of speaking, vindicated.

Noble savages? Whether the appellation is accurate, the conduct of the newborn technological savages of the West has placed such language in question. But beyond doubt, the adjective is proven accurate in a hundred ways. How lucky I am to have become the friend of our Indians in so short a time, and so easily!

Saturday, June 1. Between takes, we took off, Jeremy, his son Sam, and I, in a borrowed dugout downstream on the Don Diego. Shortly we heard a mysterious thunder; then around a gentle bend, we caught sight of the sea! A cascade of surf wide as the river mouth and stretching along, as we emerged, the countless miles of the Caribbean shore. Transfixed, struck dumb. River and ocean!

Even if I had suspected, as Jeremy did, that we were within striking distance of open sea, there was still this blazing epiphany, as contrasted with a mere glimpse at a map. I thought of my first sight of an Alaskan glacier and my first volcano in southern Chile. Sights to nourish one for a lifetime—and beyond.

> Uncertain we were
> whether parable and fact were one.
> River and ocean made together
> marriage processional,
> mystic joining of hands.
> The Don Diego curved like a bent bow,
> shot us under summoning drums
> into full sight and majesty.
>
> The mythic being
> received, like arms to breast
> time, river, ourselves riding time and river—
> into, we knew and knew not
> what—the vast sun-reddened
> artery of all.

Another adventure. Our young Swiss actor, Rolf, offered to guide us on the four-hour trek up to a lost village of the Taironas. The first hour was fairly easy through level jungle. Then started the test: three hours up the rocky face.

So we viewed firsthand the labor of an ancient people who had hewn this marvel out of virgin rock. They had bridged chasms, always with native stone, tunneled through rock, upended enormous boulders, shaped them to hold an im-

mense horizontal weight. We crawled through stone needles'
eyes, walked gingerly upon stone bridges, clattered over steps
unevenly and cunningly placed so that when trodden on, their
sharp report might warn of the approach of stranger or
enemy.

On Rolf's invitation, each of us chewed a lump of coca
leaves to relieve exhaustion and hunger, thus, I suppose, imitat-
ing the ancestors who bore the brunt of the labor, the altitude,
the long marches. In our case, I can report that it worked; the
effect was something like that of strong coffee or tea and pro-
duced a slight, gentle "high," not striking or noticeable, the air
being thin and the lungs straining.

So we arrived at the summit fairly refreshed. After the hours
of strenuous effort, we felt no hunger, so we offered our food
to an impoverished Indian family, a mother and three big-eyed
children whom we came on, camping disconsolately in a rickety
hut near the remains of the village.

Walked thoughtful and solitary amid the bones and stones
of history, thinking long thoughts induced by ghosts and hints,
thoughts of greatness and mortality, the folly and grandeur of
human endeavor, including, with all hope, the outcome of our
own.

Then down and down, mercifully by an easier route, to hear
the distant sea, and to be sweetly cheated, taking sound for
proximity. Then to be undeceived as we lost the thunders once
more.

Purity of distance. We caught sight through the under-
growth, of a watery sky, or skyey water, an indistinguishable
blinding sheet that enveloped the world and met the heavens.
Then at long last, level ground, salt spray on the face—the sea,
the sea!

Descending laboriously
the lost mountain village
round, round the cone our travail,
tracing a rune on the wild secret face.
We heard the sea
then lost the sea
then saw it face to face—
delight of sense, loss of delight.
Not yet not yet
in exhausted end
to see and hear and taste. O more to
swim in beatitude.

Sometimes a dreadful complication of a simple thing brings unwonted depression of spirit. Tonight, for instance, we five Jesuits were filmed standing around a campfire. It was the end of a (fictionally) cruel day on the jungle trail. There we gathered, to recite our night prayers.

So far, so simple. But more was to come. I imagine there are three stages of such an occurrence, as it lodges in memory.

In the first, only the event itself; firelight, the sound of water bickering and sliding along, the light of fire on the faces.

Then, as news reaches Europe and America, the simple event is shaken with tremors of romantic fantasy. The tropics, the bizarre natives, our heroic ambassadors of God! Now the lives of the missioners assume an aura of purity and heroism, a kind of transfigured distancing, in contrast to the domestic banality of life in the temperate zone of Europe.

Finally, a movie. Now technique brings romantic yearnings to an apogee. Shades of Rousseau and the Frenchman in Tahiti and the libertine in Montmartre and the Dutchman on the Côte d'Azur! Arterial coils, tubes, ventricles, cables, switches, carbon lights, filters, hidden mikes, all the etceteras of the technological storehouse are placed around a simple campfire. In fact, the technique is thrust within the fire itself; the flames can be gassed up or banked down because a gas jet is placed under the logs and controls their burning.

Meantime, entire squads of workers stand motionless in water up to their knees, having laid the cables, bickered over placement of lights, signaled to one another over considerable distances with the help of walkie-talkies, ordered silence in gravelly tones . . . And all this is repeated over and over, for some four or five hours. The cameras inch closer over the waters, to the very nimbus of the fire; the faces of the actors are halved in light. It is as though in the outer darkness, a welter of human eyes were hungering two inches away from the eyeballs and epidermis of the actors.

And finally, the finish; the set collapses, the generators cough into silence, the workers tramp wetly onto dry land, and a curious cavalcade streams out of the jungle. The circus is leaving town.

So we sped home, with our light cargo of illusion, our soporifics and highs.

A day off. People quietly reading or dozing in the sun. And suddenly the hotel garden resembles an armed camp. Eight or nine young soldiers are stalking about, each with a particularly lethal-looking weapon. Everyone starts up and takes alarmed notice.

One soldier settles in, quite at home; he lounges at the outdoor bar, gun across his lap. Then a squad appears; they process along the edge of the pool, guns and more guns. We seek out the production office to inquire what this may mean, and are told precisely nothing.

It develops later, the military have come in to patrol the

beach and prevent further dynamiting of fish. We are not comforted. Why this free and easy access of government violence to our dwelling?

Saturday, June 8. The crew has constructed an ingenious and handsome bridge at the landing stage of the river. An immense tree was felled nicely, then anchored and planed along the upper surface for a walkway.

Most of the morning is consumed in setting up a complicated shot. It requires not only a track camera ashore, but another in the river. Then the boats must come down the rapids, turn about precisely, and gently nudge and maneuver sideways into the dock.

We left the hotel at 6:30 A.M. as usual and had a fine breakfast on arrival at the set: whole-wheat bread, bacon and beans, fruit, and coffee. Then two hours of waiting. Without this diary to scribble and a good book or two, time would indeed hang heavy and limp. Poems occur, letters arrive from home (though the gap of time between their dispatch and arrival seems at times like a yawn of the Grand Canyon).

Our first real mishap of the tour. We were filming the arrival of the little fleet at the mission. The river had risen precipitously during the night; the landing stage was a welter, wildly churning.

The first instructions issued us were sketchy indeed. In consequence, our dugouts piled up dangerously, unmanageable even by our skilled Indian navigators. During an early take, two canoes capsized, including mine. I was pitched backward, cassock and all, into the fast-running current, losing my reading glasses in the bargain.

We repeated the shot four more times, and it went without

travail. A heart-stopping scene, the boats running fast. Then, on our great trunk of a bridge, spanning the high waters, some fifty Indians, children and women and men, lined up. Loud cries of joyous welcome. I sensed an enormous sigh of relief on the part of all, as we feebly tottered out of the boats.

De Niro was quite shaken by the episode; he sensibly demanded more care and better direction for the future. Also our dear Enrico, the costumer, promises to replace my spectacles this evening, an enormous relief to an obsessive reader.

The afternoon promises to be more sedate, as we film the ceremonial welcome of the missioners into the village.

Monday, June 10. There's an element of improvising the work, which I find most engaging, part of a larger atmosphere of good feeling. De Niro, shy as he is, comes across in his own way. On our last free day, he took the Indian children boating and surfing and arranged a splendid lunch for us all.

Sandy, from London headquarters, avers that our good progress is due to Roland, "a strong presence at the center of things." I credit the same gentleman, but for other reasons. Indeed, sometimes my admiration is dampened with a slight dose of exasperation. Normally quite taciturn, he sets up main lines, concentrates on the larger scope, such as our spectacular entrance into the mission and the welcome by the Indians. As for the strictly Jesuit parts, he insists on our developing them for ourselves. Feel the scene out, register it intensely, make it your own. I find this easier as I gain confidence.

Another difficulty is built into the nature of filming itself and, I surmise, would arise in any such project. We constantly undertake scenes that demand large changes of mood because they are entirely out of sequence. For instance, we must first reflect the exhilaration of our welcome by the Indians, then immediately record sorrow and shock as Altimirano announces his decision against the mission before the outraged Indians and ourselves in the priests' dining room.

Our sailing remains relatively smooth, despite all. One element that tempers the contrary winds, is undoubtedly a sense that everything in the film hinges on discipline and restraint. And one must add, we are greatly helped by the Eucharist which some of us celebrate weekly.

Reading: *Breaking Bread*, a history of the Catholic Worker, exhaustive, fascinating, only now and then pedantic. Also, *Nicholas Nickleby* and *A Hundred Years of Solitude.* Also periodicals courtesy of the 98 Street Jesuits: *Catholic Reporter, Commonweal, Sojourners, Catholic Worker.*

Meantime, our survival on the considerable run from hotel to river each day is a matter that might be termed, without equivocation, miraculous. On Thursday, one of our cars was stopped by army personnel, who stepped in with their rifles and instructed the driver to continue down the road. A mile beyond, a man lay dead in the road, shot in the head. A violent country, violent tools, vehicles, and guns.

Tuesday, June 11. Departure as usual, at dawn. A hard and important day ahead; according to our story, it seals the fate of the mission. We arrive. The lovely dwellings and church stand veiled in mist, the implacable jungle growth pushing along, pushing up. The birds sound improbably metallic, as though their song were no celebration of sunrise, but a warning off of predators.

The Indians arrive in force. It will bear observing that the men are invariably superb physical specimens, while many of the women are, in great contrast, prematurely aged, by all accounts, from prodigious childbearing. Perhaps another clue is their grief for the loss of so many children; I am informed that two of every three children die in infancy.

There is good news too. All six children born in the temporary village have survived. There is much to be said for the presence of a European doctor.

When a birth is imminent, I am told, a tent of bark is assembled inside the single-room home. Mother and midwife go in. Life in the house proceeds as usual. The mother brings forth and is back "on duty" within hours. One notes that the men have very little to do with the rearing or care of children. When a holiday occurs, they pass the day lounging, hunting, and talking.

We continue to fret and furrow our brows over Bolt's ending to the film. We seem stuck, at least for the nonce, in our own sequestered minds. Still, I suspect we're beginning to see a crack of light at last.

We must question the pieties relentlessly. Is Gabriel to be a "hero and martyr" in some debased Nietzschian sense, or a despairing one à la Camus? Or is he not rather called to act in a politically responsible way, as one who believes that dying well implies in the best instance public meaning, and therefore requires a sense of public responsibility?

We have to get him out of church, where the author had condemned him to a kind of Catholic *Götterdämmerung.* Not away from the church, but out of the church. Martin Luther King's phrase, the church is "the place you go from . . . " A place to be sure, and a community, a shelter, a source and resource—to go from. Which is to say, to face the world with faith and hope and prayer and the breaking of bread.

And thereby to offer the world a resource superior to the

world, so that the world may cease being itself—violent, intractable, untruthful, and blind.

Or if the world is determined to be itself, then Gabriel's "going forth" will make the fact publicly evident. He will not be destroyed in secret or in hiding. His death will be a political act, which is to say, responsible, accountable.

Friday, June 14. De Niro questioned me closely as he approached a difficult scene with Jeremy. Mendoza, already a Jesuit novice, informs Father Gabriel that he is resolved to take up arms to defend the Indians.

De Niro: "What was your novitiate like?"

I had to dredge back. "The Father master used to test us periodically, saying things like, 'I don't think you have this vocation, but go to the chapel and pray over it and come back and tell me what you learned.'

"I would go and do as I was told and come back, almost in tears, saying, 'I won't go, I'm staying.'

"I think his tactic was to give one a boot, to get one over a hump. He had an uncanny sense when something was being held back, when one was riding easy, on a plateau."

De Niro: "What was it in Jesuit life that you so clung to?"

"It was the life itself, and how can one describe that? It was friendship, community, the promise of support for one another, a vision of great work to be done, which those before you had done so well . . . The alternative, returning to the world, had no real attraction. But I think it all came down to my conscience versus the testing, which, by the way, was never presented as the direct command, 'You must leave.' "

A closer instance, I suggested, to the dilemma faced by Mendoza was that of the Jesuit of Nicaragua, Fernando Cardenal, who was ordered directly by his superior either to leave his government post or leave the Order. He chose to stay at his post, explaining his action as one of conscientious inability to do otherwise.

The outcome was a disaster from any sane or Christian point of view, but still somewhat mitigated. Cardenal continues to live with a Jesuit community; further, he has the option, when his government service is ended, of returning to the Jesuits.

The choice in Mendoza's case (as in Father Gabriel's) is quite simple—how is one to die? Either with gun in hand, or (as we've labored long and hard to make Gabriel credible) with sacrament in hand. Both die with the people. The choices in either case are not large, but in any Christian sense they are worlds apart.

I set down these notes in De Niro's thatched hut, a hermitage built for him to retire to between takes. It's furnished with hammock, desk, chair, and electric fan. He's on the set nearby, working away at the difficult scene with Irons. Indeed, the value and moral weight of the film depend on the moments these two struggle with. Nothing can replace them, not money, pageants, music, revelry, or the carnage of battle.

It consoles me that this wrestling with the principalities and powers, which the film portrays, is going on at home also, in the courts and prisons, the protagonists being those closest to me in life. Thought of them and thought of the struggle we undergo to get the film right—and find the two mysteriously joined.

Without such moral agony, dramatized in scenes such as this, deceptively simple, one to one, time consuming (for a few minutes a whole day expended)—without these, the film becomes a fretful, empty, period piece, just like a hundred others, distracting and inhuman.

They've been at the scene for eight hours and are still not finished. Roland is relentless.

A most complicated day, not unraveled yet.

Somebody yesterday used the word "charisma" to describe the Indians. The scene after nightfall would encourage some such description. Around the campfires, the Indians between takes improvised games, laughed, scoffed, and mimicked. At times the uncomfortable thought arose in me that they were mimicking, even gently scoffing at us!

An inviting contrast occurred to me, weary and steamy and stifled, as a subaltern kept blowing his smoke machine in my direction: the contrast between the Indians and ourselves. Makers and movers of images, we appear exhausted and harassed, even as we made moonlight in a moonless sky, rolled the all-seeing Eye about regally on its noiseless joints and wheels, made smoke from a can, made wood fires from gas tanks, made Jesuits of almost anyone, made heroes and villains and soldiers— made the world presumably, at least that momentary, many-splendored world of the film.

Charisma? I thought it too easy a word. It has overtones or undertones, on our lips, of a kind of half-witted innocence, or "not like us," meaning "a little below us."

The Indians are surely innocent, in a way that defies spaces and boundaries, properties and appetites, technique and violence. They are also unlike the Colombians, who are sorrowfully underfed and pitiful in their skeletal shambling about. (Probably many of them have TB, says the doctor.) They line up for meals like the starving street people at the Catholic Worker in New York or Chicago or anywhere. The wretched of the earth, or not so much of the earth as of the system.

The Indians seem perfectly attuned to the earth. One could never think to apply to them the word "victim"; it simply does not signify. And yet in the Chaco, in their own villages, they lack nearly all medical and dental care and are regarded as expendable in Colombian culture.

There's something almost monastic about them, something stable, benign, playful, mindful, ungrabbing, direct in look and speech. Their treatment of us is marked by a respect that brings out the best we can muster of our own dignity.

There was suddenly an end of charisma last night, about 9:30 P.M. The Indians, evidently by predesign, stopped the work dead in its tracks.

Before we quite knew what was happening, the men were in a circle under the kliegs. Of all of us, only Peter, who has lived in their village, was admitted to the caucus. It developed that they were furious—at the lateness of the hour, the wearisome, repetitive shooting of scenes involving the small children, mothers, and old folk, who should have been long since in their beds. They were also angry at the violation of their contract, according to which their work should have been agreeably completed days before.

Therefore, more money for more work. Or else . . . Peter was able finally to gain a stay of the threatened strike, but only a stay. He must win some concessions from the moguls, and soon.

Speaking of strikes, a general one is announced across Colombia. All of us in consequence are "campused" for the day, a chance to rest and catch up.

Roland tells me he's accepted in principle my version of the final scene of the film.

Our progress regarding this vexed question went something like this. First, we started with Bolt's script. Two Jesuits go off to fight in company with the resisting Indians. Two others, including myself (Father Sebastian), submit to the orders of Altimirano, under threat of excommunication, and return to Asunción. Gabriel perishes in his mission church, trapped with faithful Indians as the roof literally falls in. All this, we concluded, would never do.

Then we tried: in the style of Martin Luther King and Gandhi, Gabriel is extricated from a passive fate. He takes in hand his life and the lives of his people and leaves the mission church in procession bearing the Blessed Sacrament (as in a plague or other catastrophe in nature). So doing, he confronts the worst and evokes the best in the massed adversaries, renegade Indians, and mercenaries.

A difficulty, which I consider central, remains. The Jesuits have left Gabriel to a solitary fate, under obedience. They do this in spite of all the talk, prayer, and images of community that have preceded, creating as they have a strong impression that the priests are bonded one to another in life and death.

So we try: Sebastian (myself) has been filmed in company with another Jesuit, Alfredo, sorrowfully packing up. I propose that Sebastian change his mind, remain with Gabriel, and be seen at the end assisting in the procession. This seems to me consistent. (I'm also haunted by the photo of the priest shot in a street of Belfast, in Northern Ireland. Another priest braved the fire to bless and anoint, and he himself was killed in turn. This could be adapted with considerable power, I think.)

Cultural Note of Little Moment. "You're our guests. Why not screw you?" A letter to the United States costs forty pesos. The hotel has no stamps for sale, nor does the town. But the hotel will mail a letter—for sixty pesos. I inquired with sweetness and venom, "The heavy surcharge is perhaps for spit?"

*　　*　　*

Friday, June 21. They're making ready at the mission for the big burning that is to end the film. One feels at least a dark inkling of the original tragedy, the destruction of hopes too large, too generous, too "ahead of the times"—except that they were in fact the best and ideal realization of those times (or of ours), being simply and clearly prohuman.

"The times." What a multitude of crimes, infamies, deceptions, fantasies, and obsessions the phrase glosses over! Considering how "the times" dispose of ideal and hopeful things, must they not be regarded, then as now (as indeed we are instructed by our Bible) as simply "evil"? Which is to say, blind to human understanding, dead to compassion?

So the mission perished. As the best-laid plans and hopes of Jesuits always have perished, whether in China, India, or Paraguay. One mourns, but one also knows that this genius that invites destruction has no acceptable alternatives, anymore than the gospel has, whose divine Protagonist, we are told, also spoke the unpalatable truth, and so invited destruction.

Our film is at its best when it sticks close to those emotions and actions humans excel at or are worst at and visualizes these adequately, honestly, even clumsily, but with soul.

And the film is at its worst when it gets too big for its own good, reaches for the merely spectacular. Something of this, I think, infected today's shots, which were filled with bad smells, burning rubber, and big bangs from phony guns.

It all adds up, not in the sense of sound mathematics, but in heaps of inert debris, whether of dummy corpses in costume, or smoking tires, or the rooftree caving in.

When in contrast things come together and cling in the mind and heart, it is invariably because of one or two faces, a gesture, a few words uttered as though meant, received as though heard. Even a moment of this is a healing; it enables one, so to speak, to take up his pallet and walk again.

Saturday, June 22. One of those days. It struck me in the midst of waiting, wandering about, pursued by a very cloud of blood-sucking fleas (they hum about one, appetitive, like an eighth plague of Egypt) that I could never again take part in such an enterprise as this. Is it merely the disaffection and wear and tear induced by jungle weather? Or is it a gleam of the truth that ordinarily one sails past, ears stopped, lashed to a mast by routine and inertia?

In any case, the work, the crew, the scope and outlay and swamping of ends by means—the Machine preempting—these cross my grain like a saw on a nail. Too big, too overweening, too possessive for that comfort we name strength.

Our situation at home is afflicting, the need of a consistent voice and presence. In light of these, my months here appear as too frivolous for ease of mind.

A "down" mood has its symbol at hand, in fact plenty of them. One that bumps along in the mind is the huge mound of plastic garbage that is trotted away each day—testimony of our rain forest revels—taken to God knows where, but surely not to be degraded naturally and spread on growing fields.

Killing fields? They stretch wide and far in the mind.

Not always, and by no means everywhere, are the details of the film under control. Almost always, almost everywhere, but not quite. Yesterday Puttnam wrote me a note. Since I was departing for home prior to the windup of the Great Mission Episode, I would not be required for any portion of the scene, even for its inception. "But please come out tomorrow and view the mission; you'll love it." Which I did, and did indeed.

All afternoon I wandered about in the heat and light, in a very stupor of admiration—the scope of it, the delicacy and geometry, like an embodiment of celestial law, a sublimely ordered architectural universe.

And all through the afternoon, I was receiving contrary signals from young John, the runner. One time it would be, "Dress up in Jesuit garb; you're on." Then again, "Instruction canceled." And then, "Let me check with Roland." Finally, "Roland wants you; you're on."

Thursday, June 27. Toward evening. A most enchanting scene takes form. Some fifteen hundred Indians gather before the church of the Great Mission, patient and silent and self-composed. For hours, prior to the signal that sets them in movement, they had endured the 110-degree midday heat, standing in the sparse shade of a grove of trees.

Then toward a magnificently lucid sunset, they formed a procession and began to pass, single file, up the slight incline of the parade ground toward the church; old folks, children, women carrying babies. They divided off into ranks, those in the front row with backs to the church; the arrangement allowed for an open aisle down the middle. Candles were distributed and lighted, and all were seated on the ground—dark heads, black sleek fall of hair, woven shifts of creamy white.

Then, "Camera! Roll it! Action!" I was being smoked to a fare-thee-well near one of the campfires. De Niro and Liam Neeson, the young Irishman, stood nearby, two or three children playing at their feet. Out of the doorway, fleet and graceful, Gabriel passes. Candles in hand, the Indian ranks rise in greeting like a marvelous wave of light. Up and away he walks toward the church portal, where a group of Jesuits wait to greet him. They pass indoors together.

The whole episode consumed perhaps four minutes. It had been prepared for all day.

I am to depart for New York early next morning. Hearing this, De Niro quietly arranges a farewell party at one of the colonial houses of Cartagena transformed into a splendid restaurant.

He gets the word about. Roland and all the actors are in attendance. Sinead and Jeremy, Roland and Cheri, Toukie and Robert, Mirella, the Italian photographer, Chuck Low, Liam and Ian. Roland favored us with the words of a song, Jeremy the music, which he played on a guitar. I record here the verse of gentle delightful kitsch:

> Here's a song to Daniel Berrigan.
> When, where will we see him again?
> If we do, we'll tell and tell again
> Loving tales of Daniel Berrigan.
> Cause if he's ill we'd wish him well again.
> That's the charm of Daniel Berrigan.
> Let's pray he sinks a nuclear sub again.
> All his fights he'll win and win again.
> Our very special Daniel Berrigan.

They concocted a potion and named it instantly Loyola Punch, a mysterious essence of vodka and fruit juice. Full glasses of this ambrosial draught arrived on a tray with a gentle light in the midst. A sight (and savor) for the gods. Glorious, as was the whole evening!

We said farewell. Jeremy embraced me, "It will be a different film because of you."

I tergiversated in a shrugging, Irish way, but nonetheless I was pleased as a cat at the cow's teat, "All I did was twitch an altar cloth now and then, some ridiculous detail or other."

But he was, of course, correct.

And so farewell for a time, as I voyage from the Land of Undoing, homeward to the Land of Unknowing.

The months in Colombia undoubtedly had the severest limitations built in; these remain with me, a shadow over so revelatory a time. Especially the mandarin style—good food, the best hotels. This is a cause of shame and unease, something I tried to mitigate at least a little by fasting and prayer.

I'm chagrined that our (my) exposure to the poor was only by way of a kind of compassionate tourism—an oxymoron if ever one was coined. Simply, we visited the poor rather than lived with them. Young Rolf, our Swiss "Jesuit" actor, put this another way: "You actors should have spent the months here living among the Indians, instead of being tucked away in your compound." And of course he was right, in principle and except for an undeniable fact—few of us could have survived that primitive life. More, a question arises: would it have been just to inflict so undisciplined a crew as ours on their traditional discipline and innocence? I doubt it would have been.

The beauty of the gift quite overwhelms me, these wondrous, difficult, frustrating, fiery, icy three months. They were not merely a respite, a laying aside of burdens (but by no means all burdens—our people on trial and in prison, Nicaragua, the Reagan plague). It was also a respite in time. I was allowed to taste and touch the past—past heroism, joy, perseverance, betrayal—and what came of all this. The Jesuits, dead and buried by collusion of church and state, rose once more in the world, contrary to the wildest expectation some fifty years after the destruction.

They had submitted to their tragedy; the creators of utopia

died in disgrace, many of them in chains. And I wonder how many of those who were carted away like detested slaves to European prisons thought in their prophetic souls that something, after all, would come of this. Did a few so think, or perhaps only one?

Sunday, August 4–Monday, August 5. New York to Iguaçu, Argentina.

Altitudinous Thoughts en Route.

"If you do not stand by Me, you will not stand at all" (Isa. 7:9).

"Why are you so anxious to die?" (Ezek. 18:31).

"What will the arms race look like in A.D. 2000?" (Sölle). (What will the earth look like? What will we look like? What will Christ look like—to us?)

"For the world to continue, brains must be washed; so must hands" (Anon.).

"If we want to own things we must also have weapons. From this came all the quarrels and battles that make love impossible. And this is why we refuse to own anything" (Francis of Assisi).

"We cast our lot with life, even if it meant death. . . . Happiness we have known, it was present everywhere, with women, men, children, wherever real resistance was being offered" (Carmen Castillo, Santiago, 1981).

"To draw Him into our flesh" (Luther).

"Prison—not the most I can do. The least I can do" (Anon.).

*   *   *

Tuesday, August 6. Hiroshima Day. Iguaçu. Ironic, even dismaying to the spirit, that I be here, surrounded by the majestic beauty of the waterfall, while Phil and Jerry are probably being arrested on the anniversary of the bomb. The best I can manage by way of solidarity with them and so many others is a day of solitude and a bit of fasting and prayer.

> Hiroshima Day. I remember
> at Iguaçu the waterfall, a moveable
> unmoving feast for the eye.
> Gigantic, thunderous, proclaiming
> the glory of God, the advent
> of hierophants of the last hour.
> Not warriors; witnesses
> standing watch perpetually
> as the world pitches over, a suicide.
> Or angels, and the tomb's mouth
> empty of death, a house of honeycomb.

Our crew of dreamers and doers is all but assembled; we start the shoot tomorrow. Last night, a somewhat muzzy supper discussion with Liam and Bob and young Dan. Are films something more than another block in the consumer imagination, a further debilitation of already exhausted spirit? I had raised like questions at home (some would say ad nauseam).

It was reassuring to hear that yes, such and such a film had made a difference in the direction life took. This was all greatly helpful, though our conversation might be as an instance of *parti pris*, since my friends have what might be called a vested interest in voting that good times follow on their efforts. Still I tend to respect them as rather cool and canny types.

*   *   *

Trying to spend this holy and tragic anniversary in solitude, in a country still occupied in sorting out the debris of recent crimes in high places. But who will be so fond as to think that the criminals who obliterated Hiroshima will ever be brought to justice? In a hellish parody of the consecrated phrase, they "rest in peace." They died as they lived—beyond accountability. Yet the Psalmist warns (or promises?), "There is One who judges."

Reading Romero's biography and Etty Hellman's diaries. Quite a heady diet.

Jeremy arrived, big grin intact, though he looks travel worn, having been on the road and in the air for the intervening month. He reports a miraculously beautiful trip from Colombia with son Sam and tutor Ian.

Awakened at dawn by the thunderous waterfalls. And the first blessing of my eyes is the innocent mist. It rises as though from some cauldron of creation, a tease of the spirit weaving in and out of the gorges. Then the sun takes command, that planet of logic and clarity, armed with calipers and second sight. To set things right? But they were right, shrouded first in darkness, then in predawn, awaiting a name, a summoning. Perhaps the sun comes on such a scene only to define the exact geometrics of mystery?

> The falling waters bespeak majesty
> unwearied, bespeak the heart
> perpetually receiving, giving forth—
> or a mouth-to-mouth respiration, kiss
> of life to life.
> Peremptory death rebuked, death
> tossed, tumbled, sport and spoils of those waters.
>
> Then celebrational soul!
> as though time broke a rainbow

> wondrously to bits—a cloud of butterflies
> announces a higher god.
> Wings like a hand's feathery touch
> linger in my hand.
> Covenant, promise, fidelity.

Then the offensive clatter and chatter of the copters started up, transporting equipment and food from the hotel to the falls.

Thursday, August 8. We worked all morning, cold and drenched under the great waterfall. Everyone bore up well in good spirit. But news got about that Jeremy had had a close call yesterday on the rock face. My blood ran cold to hear of it. It seemed he lost foothold momentarily when a rock fragment gave way, and for several seconds, he held on over the void only by his hands.

This it seemed to me was gross negligence on the part of someone, since stunt climbers and doubles are all over the place. Surely the actors should refuse to take chances that in their inexperience could cost life and limb. Liam agrees with me in his straight-faced Irish way, though I note a slight gap between noble sentiment and actual practice in his case too.

In any case. Domestic as hell, I squat here on a precipitous hillside; the waterfall utters its thunders. I'm drenched and swathed in towels, courtesy of Gold Crest Studios.

> We clambered upward in jungle mud,
> fell flat, stood once more.
> Cold, cold as the waters
> that drenched us with green hell.
> Jeremy gasped, "What men they were,
> those Jesuits
> who dared it first, no all-seeing eye
> publishing them to the world."

Yes, but no world
hectoring them either.
No Nicaragua
raining its fall of blood on their backs.
Only calabashes, hammocks, cases,
and the light yoke of the Gospel.
Then the mickmockery of macaws
scrambling the plain command—
The harsh and dreadful word called love.

The copters natter overhead. Slung beneath one of these iron insects like an obscene egg sac is the penitential burden of Mendoza.

Later De Niro and Liam are laboring over their difficult and passionate roles. Mendoza drags himself uphill in the mud and filth. Fielding, at wits' end, suddenly lunges forward, whirls his machete, and cuts that hideous umbilical of damnation. The burden falls away, but not for long.

Mendoza is furious; murder glares in his eyes. He passes Fielding, fist upraised, scrambles downhill once more to recover his burden. Carry that weight, a long time.

I can imagine, even at this remove of time, the tensions that built up on that proving ground where, perennially, Jesuit authorities and subjects take one another's measure.

According to our script, Gabriel refused to interfere so long as Mendoza was determined to drag his affliction along. So Fielding took matters into his own hands. Admirable, but no lasting relief.

Long delightful dinner with Liam, young Dan, the trainer Roland, Bob, and Bob's son Rafael. De Niro invited me to sojourn with him and his entourage for a few days in Buenos Aires after we finish our stint here. We'll see.

*　　*　　*

Reading the life of Archbishop Romero, I'm astonished and afflicted to realize the depth of persecution he underwent in his last years, not only from the bishops of Nicaragua, but from Rome. I was proud to read how the Jesuits stood by him and suffered like calumnies and threats.

I keep marveling, like a changeling from another planet, at being here in this extraordinary setting. Perhaps it's an instance of a general bewilderment that I'm still on earth at all.

Last night the phone rang toward midnight. Carol from Syracuse, clear as a struck bell. And the good news—Jerry was not arrested on Hiroshima Day. The group of protesters painted "shadow people" to commemorate the unspeakable crime, the vaporizing of Japanese under the bomb. Their action was illegal of course, at the entrance of the Air Force base, but authorities were chary of public notice and chose to ignore the whole matter.

Still no word of how Phil fared at the Pentagon. I keep hoping, in my lily-livered way, that he is not locked up.

Monday, August 12. Another call from the States assures me. Both Phil and Jerry are out of jail. I suppose my sigh of absolute joy could be heard above the trumpets of the Iguaçu.

I hardly know how to define my feelings in such matters. On the one hand, I confess to the absolute necessity of trying to keep pushing the peace ball up the Sisyphean slope; on the other, a sense of dread and sorrow awakens, when those I love are, yet once more, consigned to durance vile.

Meantime back at the dream factory. Joffé and Puttnam, who might reasonably be expected to face the Second Coming unflapped, are delighted with the work so far accomplished here. They understate delight of course, but all the same, they smile away like cats in a vat of cream. A few things will have to be gone over, nothing unusual in so complex an undertaking, notably the conversion scene between Gabriel and Mendoza in the Hospital for Incurables and the final scene, the burning of Gabriel's mission and his death. It appears that the fires got out of hand, the Indians (understandably) panicked and surrounded Jeremy, and he fell out of range of the cameras.

These two will be redone, the first in London, and the second here in Iguaçu.

Yesterday Jeremy and I drove into Paraguay. The border city is named for the abominable Stroessner, as are the airport in Asunción and many public buildings. The border town is a tacky free-for-all. It's almost impossible to gain a sense of the Paraguayan people, with Brazilians, Argentinians, Chinese, and Japanese milling about, the stores jammed with gimcrackery, electronics, booze, clothing—a sight seen nowhere else in Latin America, at least to my voyaging eyes.

Stroessner is the last (thanks to the gods of irony and lightning) of the billionaire pirates and breakers of bones. The cream of everything exchanged in the country is said to go into his coffers. I said to Jeremy, "The atmosphere here turns one into a swine. One should snoop about on all fours, going 'oink, oink.'"

De Niro's little son Rafael is bounding about the premises, having an electric good time with the Indian kids. No language troubles here. They rassle and romp, the one with no Spanish, the others equally innocent of English.

*　　*　　*

Frenetic technical activities keep the day humming, followed by endless waiting about on the pleasure of the Machine. Meantime the copters buzz overhead, trailing great sacks of equipment.

Our Argentinian workers are pretty much on the model of those we hired in Colombia. Skinny to the point of attenuation, they clamber about the rocks, carrying impossible burdens; they go up and down the perilous walkways, across the rapids in rubber boats. They are our only inkling and invasion of the vast misery and hunger of Argentina, and beyond. The sight makes for thoughtfulness, then for considerable angst—presuming of course that one is not merely sleepwalking in the day.

A sodden morning turns about, sheerly brilliant, then grey. The opulent waters put on a sudden golden face; then they brown off, but they're always turbulent and threatening. Bob, Liam, and Rolf have a difficult swimming scene, where they are pursued by a hundred mercenaries and Indians. They're nothing short of heroic, launching out on the rapids with no protection from the tooth of the wind.

I wish there were something engaging to report. But the copters keep gnawing away at one's nerves, violating all natural sound with their horrible grinding of molars or gears.

Some incomprehensible activity is going on between a few actors and the director and makeup artists; it's as though a queen bee were being stroked and preened. The crowd of extras idles about, passing time. I've been accoutred in this filthy blanket all day, without being summoned to earn a peso.

The weather stays uncertain, and so keeps everyone on edge, between sweat and chills. Although I brought along Kafka's diaries and a camera, neither brings solace. Yet I keep warm the memory of last night's phone call, clear and near, as Jerry and Carol conveyed the good news: everybody arrested is out of jail. That alone makes today bearable.

The rainbow over the falls, a habitual miracle, catches the breath. But how to describe what transpired a few minutes ago? We stand and work in the shadow of a receding winter sun, then, on the distant Brazilian side of the falls, it is as though a god's eye opened from sleep. The entire space over the water, covering the height and breadth of the vast horseshoe, grew radiant and shimmered; a spectrum arose, distinct bands of color, as though a patina had been stirred gently, then aerated; the most delicate green-azure imaginable, gently yielded to gold, then deepened to carmine. Earth and water a single bowl, and color itself distilled to an essence at once unearthly, solemn, and unutterably joyous.

Who could dwell on wickedness or evil after such a gift? We held our breaths. The conflict of the screenplay seemed to grow unseemly. The faces of actors, in whom evil and malice mingled, were momentarily transfigured. Then back to business. The falls are, after all and in a manner of speaking, another matter than the Fall.

Tuesday, August 13. Reading the liberation theologians of Latin America, with varied reactions. Some are admirably modest and tentative, virtues I believe should be conspicuous when one ventures to "theologize" about one's own times, opaque as they are, and apt for all sorts of notions to be cast into the air—like dust miming gold dust.

God knows we are dust, gifted or cursed with pretensions to become something better, gifted with certain graces to be made into something better.

But it seems to me that certain of the liberationists are as tempted as anyone else to become obsessive Pelagians—theorists of the "one way," our way. Jargon is a rather accurate sign that the dust of Pelagianism is in the air, as though "liberation," understood in all manner of idealistic, cultural, economic, or quasi-military ways, were equivalent to the banishment of original sin and sinful structures.

I set this down, conscious as I try to be, that the developments in the Nicaraguan church and society are far more biblically true to love of God and neighbor than the piratical politics of the United States. I am conscious, too, that our sinful inertia of spirit and gargantuan selfishness inevitably ricochet off the flesh of the poor elsewhere.

So we too proceed, as do all mortals (though certainly in unequal degree and with unequal guilt) under the sign of sin, as well as the hope of liberation from sin, groaning all the while in our bondage, our emptiness of life and love, our lives that are a kind of caricature and grimace of God's original intention for us. We can summon little hope of effecting anything of worth or moment in our world; and in this, I believe, we carry the stigma of "underdevelopment" far more visibly than the least and last of the peasants of Nicaragua.

For our base communities, we have only the Catholic Worker, Sojourners, Jonah House, a few other lights, and small ones at that, in a vast darkness. We have never had the reins of apocalypse thrust in our hands, the word shouted at us, "You're in charge. You make sense of things. Bring the world under control . . . " Nor will such an event conceivably happen in our lifetime.

So we muck along as best we might, making do; so many in prison, many serving the poor, many offering sanctuary. No big deal, no big theology, no big clout (or even little one). Crimes committed daily in high places; people pushed off the

map; power plays succeeding brilliantly; weapons multiply-
ing—all this quite as though we were not in the world, God
were not there, Christ were a myth or fetish for the weak.

When one gets down to the bone of things, we're about as
helpless as the campesinos around us in Argentina, as far as
exerting weight on the scales.

Well, as to the theologians. Once they leave the Bible, they
lose me. I don't write this to huff and puff about orthodoxy or
heterodoxy or anyone's doxy. Maybe I write about tested and
governing images versus romanticism or activism or passivism—
or any "ism" at all. A circumference requires a "still center";
and however adventurous one's exploring of the edge of things,
one must take soundings, direction, a sense of who and where
one is in the world, one's distance from the central point. Otherwise the venture becomes, so to speak, pointless.

We stumble about witlessly, selling ourselves short with
ersatz "theologizing," foreign as we are to the faith of (to make
a near point) these Jesuits of the eighteenth century. There is
a way of standing, and many ways of falling. One way seems
to be that of one theologian I'm reading: you give up on your
own tradition, which you judge useless or used up. At the same
time, those who follow another way appear more radiant, sin-
gle-minded, sacrificial (though here a great measure of romanticism hums along, à la Ernesto Cardenal).

Nor are the substitutes offered particularly reassuring; they
have an old, resuscitated smell like pantheism, Pelagianism,
reductionism, Gnosticism. And if one were to grant place to the
sublime analogy of being, they show a certain contempt and
fear of God as Person. In place of the personal God, one is
offered a sampling of the following: (and I quote) "Task,"
"Revolution," "Force," "Motivation," "Horizon," and (yes)

"Omega Point," and (I swear it) "Shining Dots," "The Great Exclamation Point," and [*sic*] "Exuberent Yes." I ask myself, in a laudable effort to identify the "fetishes" by which we live today, which we adore—do we have here anything more than a flea market of little idols, idolettes, so to speak?

I hope I do not sound contemptuous of suffering and victimized people. It is incumbent on good sense to listen with great respect and love to those who act and think and give their lives, proceeding from another tradition than ours—whether humanism or Marxism. It is quite another thing, or so it seems to me, when a well-known theologian (Juan Casanas of Spain) presents "other images" with a straight face, destitute as the images are, and partial, and even ridiculous.

Perhaps in the face of such an intellectual assault, one is required to (1) utter an act of repentance for his own welcoming of the idols, (2) evict them; new, old, all; success, security, solution, all. Thus renewing not a reality as great, difficult, and constantly betrayed as covenant—something far less; the shame, second thought, and backward glance known as Pascal's wager.

It seemed at one point taken for granted that the stunt boys were brought here to do the dangerous scenes, including the descent on ropes over the falls. Suddenly it seems I was mistaken. It evolved that Liam, Rolf, Bob, and Jeremy were hot to try the sheer descent for themselves. So a proffer was made. Would I go over? It's perfectly safe, etc.

I of course would not, not for all the pesos in Latin America or all the dollars in the World Bank.

In consequence I was much improved by spasms of humor like: "Daniel, you'll go up enormously in my estimation, if you'll agree to the descent!" To which I was moved to re-

spond equally, "Hooray for me, and too bad for your estimation . . . "

O to know that invisible point where courage sheers off into
foolishness. And the courage to stand there, this side of the
taboo.

Wednesday, August 14. Forty-six years ago today, I left my
reasonably happy home in quest of the Jesuits, little thinking
I would be sitting today thousands of miles from that home (or
any home) on a jungle cliffside, and still be, so to speak, in quest.
All the jungles, asphalt and otherwise, in between! All the years
and works and days!

The distant waters go softly as the waters of Siloe; leaves
barely turn and turn about in the gentlest of breezes. The sun
breaks through; workers come and go, lugging their tools of
trade.

In the midst of it all, myself, an observer turned actor.
Carrying along a modicum of baggage, most of life still a matter
of waiting for the main act, which only now and again pushes
one onstage. And then, only for a bit part.

> I've waited a long time
> in and out of jungles
> for I know not what—
> "That this mortal body
> put on immortality?"
>
> We wore the shabby moth-eaten robes
> that so resemble the body, its wear and tear.
> I said, "This might be the cassock
> I entered the Jesuits in."
> Now it most resembles
> a second aged skin.
> And what trump or season

will put it off; and what on earth
will I look like then?

Most dreams are mere confabulations, not worth troubling
the light of day. But last night I dreamed of my dear friend, so
recently deceased, William Stringfellow. He moved among us
preparing and serving a meal. And we, his guests, said to one
another, "How well he looks, much better than last year!"
There was also a garden, and along the curving beds, whole ears
of corn stood upright, tied to supporting stakes. That is all I
remember, but it was a great comfort.

"It is better to be silent and be, than to speak and not be"
(Ignatius of Antioch).

Reading *The Idols of Death and the God of Life*, so concerned and eloquent on the subject of idolatry, reminds me of
a strange osmosis. The same biblical theme of idols and true
worship means so much to us in our reflection groups in the
United States. One Bible, many tongues!

So we sat in the enchanted glade of the jungle. It was lunch-
time. Each found along the precipitous path a few inches of
fairly level ground. Open box lunches. Everyone's talk, Ger-
man, Spanish, Italian, English, softened, commingling with the
perpetual voice of the waters. A golden day, in more senses than
one.

It's now 2:00 P.M. Liam, Bob, and Jeremy have been on their
climb, far below us, all through the morning.

The clay along the jungle road as we come in keeps wide and
deep ditches of watery mud; they scarcely allow passage of our

pickup truck. The puddles are extremely dangerous, especially when a second lumbering pachyderm approaches ours, and both proceed to dig in with lowered horns. I can but look imploringly heavenward, hoping against hope for yet another act of God, which, as these notes testify, is indeed vouchsafed.

I catch myself wondering on this, my anniversary, something like: what is a clown like me doing, blundering about the earth?

The province (or state) where our film is being made is named for the Jesuit missions here: *Misiónes*. Last night, the bishop of the capital, Posadas, came to the hotel to greet me. He was accompanied by a Lebanese Jesuit and a handsome woman, a Doctor of Education as it turned out. They invited me to dine, things went swimmingly, though it must be reported that the Jesuit scholar blinked temperately behind his gold spectacles as though a mote had invaded his eye, when I recounted bits and pieces of our nefarious activities at home.

The bishop, with his aged nutcracker face, beamed away and said nary a word all evening. It appeared, however, that like many silent folk, he had a brain behind his eyes. He had established a protected village for some twelve hundred Guarani Indians modeled on the old Jesuit *reducciónes*. There he is careful to respect their rites and symbols and beliefs, an evangelizing patience and respect. I liked him immensely.

The woman, meticulously gotten up, appeared to be a friend of both clerics. Nor was she amused, anymore than the Jesuit, at the account, however sketchily offered, of my delicts. Indeed her calm shivered and broke like thin ice, when I made bold to mention our "crimes" during the Vietnam War. "But such things as you did allowed the Communists to take over the country!" she shrilled. I met this outburst "like a painted ship upon a painted ocean," and the skies shortly resumed their normal hue.

We began again in the intermittent rain, on a ledge some fifty feet above the rapids. At this point I could have starred in Hitchcock's *Vertigo* with Oscar-quality authenticity, quaking, shivering, clinging for dear life . . .

We take and take endlessly, all the day long, in close and at distance. After our first try Roland says, "Things are developing well," and smiles as though pleased. But toward the end (to the Indians and ourselves), "You're losing the innocence of the thing; remember, it's all about love."

So we toil on, somewhat jaded, artisans of a heroism easier practiced than reproduced; or so it seems to the reproducers, who've never been summoned by the angel of heroism, as goes without saying! Roland said to me, "If the secret of the scene is love of Jesuits for one another, including Mendoza, you should all move closer to him in this crisis, no?"

And at another point, "You're passing too easily from shock [at sight of the Indian brandishing his knife, threatening to dispatch Mendoza] to joy and wonderment that the Indian is capable of something so uncomplicated and right as the cutting of the rope [a sign exactly right, as to substance and timing, the forgiveness that heals]."

Serious talk, and at some length; indeed Roland was seeing this scene as another pivot of the film. We must offer together a credible vision, not only of death (common enough in this film and most films) but of resurrection, most difficult and uncommon both in human dealings and in art.

The scene builds, layer on layer, take after take, to an almost unbearable pitch. Mendoza, between wild laughter and wilder tears, is joined in a rush by the Jesuits, huddling and clutching him on the ledge of rock. And the Indians grow wild also with relief for the plenary act of their leader. They have cleansed Mendoza in the fire of forgiveness and can now welcome him— if not as a brother (too easy, too fast) at least as a restored human.

Sunday, 18 August. Yesterday one of our drivers, perhaps the most beloved of all, a man of great experience and compassion, was killed on the road. Evidently a tire blew, his car vaulted over and over, and he died instantly. It developed that he was driving a new car with old tires.

The loss of a life brought home to us with new force how lucky we were in Colombia, as well as here. In Argentina the driving is spectacular and the roads in spotty condition. But Colombia!—sheer insanity, broken field running!

There was a party for fifty of us to mark De Niro's birthday. They reserved a room in a family-type restaurant in Iguacu. Cockney games and humor were so broad as to evoke wincing here and there.

Today a group of us took off in wild rain for the hundred-kilometer run to the ruins of the San Ignacio Mission, after which the so-called Great Mission of the film is modeled. The following rather somber notes were undoubtedly influenced by the dour weather, as well as something one might call inner weather. In any case.

It becomes difficult to grant moral credit to the life we lead in the dream factory. It seems at times as though the stories and images we concoct for the public are not more substantial than our own fantasies. One might construct a child's game of questions and answers.

Whose every whim is speedily answered, as though by a genie in a crystal bottle? Who is it can appear or disappear on this continent or that at a snap of fingers and the roar of a jet? Who is it, down in the milk house, skimming off the cream of creation, leaving the sour whey for others less fortunate (or less inclined to thievery)?

How terrible when unease grows easy, and I begin to take in stride things that at the start appalled.

Thus today, we set out in a big bus—capacity thirty-seven—nine of us and the driver. And this conspicuous, not to say glaring or morally contemptible consumption, appeared as "normal," "our due." Which is to say, on a free day, we simply join the expensive tourism of a tiny minority of privileged, even while, as was evident through the fog and storm, the poor trudge along in the brunt of the fierce weather.

At least Rolf, that child of unspoiled clarity, helped us by urging the driver to stop for anyone along the roads who needed a lift. So we did, several times.

For myself, and despite all, I wanted to journey to San Ignacio not as a tourist, but as a pilgrim. I knew there was blood on those mute stones and a glory around them. The inevitable defeat of a work too pure for this world? Its daring astounds and invigorates; and the sacrifice that carried it through offers a true measure against which I place everything paltry and superficial in my life.

And the film. I reflect somberly that those who refuse greatness are condemned to mimic it, as though the final form of things would be a hell that was no more than a grimace and charade of heaven. But these are dark thoughts, and by no means the whole story.

We arrived finally in mist and fog, over terribly dangerous roads, in our great lumbering land animal. The environs of the mission are at least as tacky and ill-kempt and money grubbing as those of Lourdes. We passed into the parade ground, through an ornate red stone archway, on toward the Indian dwellings all of red stone, somewhat like our urban row houses, each "prefabbed" in like form and size. Each also has its covered porch, of which only stone columns remain, each with its garden space. The houses were laid out in lengthy rows of perhaps twenty dwellings each.

One stone column along a row had been entirely enveloped over the years in a living tree, like a body of stone wrapped in folds of wooden raiment. I glanced through a natural cleft in the wood and felt along with my hands; and indeed, the heart of the tree was stone.

We walked diagonally across the sward toward the church portal. The broken archway loomed up before us, wine red and the lucent green of the lawn. Indeed it was as though the wine of life had petrified there, falling and tumbling. Strangely powerful, almost ominous, the arches, like hooded twin giants or Assyrian demigods stood, each with huge legs wide apart, each accoutred in rough scales of rusted armor. The arch had toppled at its keystone; only verticals remained, twin massive columns, almost pyramidal, splendidly carved with Christian baroque and Indian motifs.

From a grey distance, the portals seemed unaccountably gouged with dark relief figures or hieroglyphs. On closer approach, these were seen indeed to be stylized angels in high and low relief, nicely balanced, profiles turned toward the center of each "obelisk." Then serpents, vines, and as we saw later—propped ignominiously against a wall and quite broken in two—the great seal of the Jesuits, carved in high relief. It had undoubtedly once adorned the keystone.

The proportions of the church were ample and splendid,

though one could no longer appraise the interior. Only the four walls, jaggedly aloft, standing only to the height of the window frames.

The priests of the mission, it was clear, were buried around the high altar, of which only a rough and ready massive stone heap remains.

We walked slowly about, rendered silent by a rainfall grown gentle and ghostly, as well as by the ghosts who haunt and hallow the ruin.

The mission well was wondrously intact.

> The sweet-water well and the sulphurous world
> that soured and wrecked—all, all save this.
> Square blocks rise like a round
> tower of Atlantis, underwater.
> Fearful too; you could pitch over
> like an empty bucket, fill to brim, sink,
> a stone in a dark pocket.
> Deep, deep as God's
> first thought of God.
> Someone cast a round mirror
> down and down
> where things begin to be.
> Faces leapt back at me,
> masks, memories, angels on guard,
> tender advocacies and vows,
> skies broken by thunderous hammers,
> days long vanished into enchantment's cave,
> auras, lives loved, lost at last.
> Everything, nothing.
> It was airy water after watery air.
> "Come down, come down,"
> the mirror whispered.
> "I promise (cross

my false heart)—
beatitude.
Kiss me
and drown."

My mind keeps reverting to the death of the driver. Wonderment mingles with gratitude for the unexplainable Providence that up to the present bus ride has kept the rest of us from a like fate. All such protection is undeserved, our own, I judge, especially so. In Colombia, we bolted off like madmen on mad horses, in those badly shod cars, as though flinging our lives to the mountain winds. It was like a *défi* cast in the teeth of the Creator, an absurd arrogance.

Yet it was only I who felt so strongly our folly, as though tempting the gods to do their worst. For the others, it was driving as usual. Brows would rise in polite astonishment, as though some creature or other born to walk upright were raising moral questions about a natural process, and all the while insisting on crawling the earth!

Thus was illustrated for me yet once more (if I am still in need of instruction) how out of step I am in the world.

Monday, August 19. Bill Wesley, the assistant director, took me by the hand (he's irreformably paternal in tender moments) to the edge of the waterfall, over the plank walkway. "Watch this closely, Danny." He stepped down, as though in pure space; but he was evidently not, for he had found a footing under the rush and foam. "You see what's here; I don't want to get wet further, but that's the idea."

And what was the idea? Why, simple enough; that on the morrow I should do this same aerated space walk for some thirty feet along the edge of existence.

I said my thanks for the trouble and pled my vertigo. And both sentiments were sincere and matter of fact.

"Thass all I want to know, Danny," and he stalked off.

Life itself tends to be quite vertiginous enough for me, thank you. I felt, moreover, in a sufficiently clear way that I wasn't born to perish for the greater glory of filmdom, that this proffered caper was eons above and beyond the call of duty. No thank you indeed.

"The verb 'to have' is the death of God" (Moacyr Felix, Brazil).

Wednesday, August 21. These drenching waterfall scenes have some of us growing fins and scales and webbed feet. Others simply cave in afterward with coughs and flu. Yesterday they had us six Jesuits do a cakewalk under the torrent, a rather hazardous procedure over slippery scattered rocks at the base, cold spray meantime drenching us to the pelt.

> We disappear under the waterfall
> as though in time. The water falls and falls;
> true time
> is in disaccord, warped; past, always past,
> a trick named time.
> The waterfall calls
> like a truthful angel, true time,
> the poetry of things; no slack prose
> (things as they are, we as we are).
> The angel commands. We disappear
> under the waterfall. Emerge
> drenched in beatitude;
> no actors, no additional souls—
> agents, conquerors, walkers of water!

At least we were relatively on sea level and not at the brink of some dizzying cliff! So we managed quite well.

They were solicitous as worker bees afterward, stripping us, wrapping us in towels and bathrobes, sending us back to the hotel to recover (but in no case supplying us with wet suits beforehand, as would have appeared sensible).

Even a hot shower in my room didn't benefit the old frame greatly; I shivered for an hour under blankets, poncho, sweater.

There was yet another long palaver at supper; these evening meals are in many ways the high spot of days that can be enervating and exhausting. Puttnam seized the baton from Jeremy, Bob, and myself. He proceeded at 78-speed to air his opinions concerning Christ. To wit, he thought him a rather unpalatable Being, all said, narrow of heart and mind, someone who in fact "gets in the way of God." I thought all this rather novel, in view of a venerable tradition among Christians and others that Christ is a kind of intense burning glass, concentrating the truth of the Father in our direction.

Even in such deadly serious matters there is no accounting for taste, which can be bizarre or merely eccentric.

A great measure of such opinion lurks offstage in shadow (a being like a prompter whispers attitudes, prejudices, longings, enticements, the dark side of each of us, filling in the words even, or secretly contradicting what is said).

None the less, we often seize occasions these days for a laugh. I have a favorite saying, which perhaps applies: the real film is proceeding outside the film.

They're having great difficulty managing the climax of the battle in the rapids. It appears that the dugout canoes have a draft of some nine inches, but the water at the falls, for all its apparent splendor and density, is only some five inches deep—

and is often even less when, as at present, no rain has fallen for days. So the canoes, some of them loaded with dummies of mercenaries, soldiers, Jesuits, Indians, simply roll along the rapids, go one-third over, and hang there with their prows in space like reneging Egyptian sun boats, refusing immortality.

I saw the dummies, a dozen or more of them, lined up in their six-foot boxes along the riverbank; they look for all the world like clay homunculi in some primitive myth, awaiting the creative breath. I thought of a clutch of ancestors, their fingers reaching out from far back in time, from pretime perhaps. In any case, something of a mythological aura surrounds them, a longer leap than the two centuries suggested by their costumes.

> They've seven dummies of a "crucified Jesuit"
> to toss over the falls. I saw them tumble
> like cheerful ships, arms soaring, oaring.
> One, headlong like a champion, thirsting
> for the finish. Another, feet braced
> loomed vertical at the brink; a momentous
> Nijinsky leap. "Farewell," he intoned,
> a priest red as sunset.
>
> Thus goes the film. Not thus life
> which alas, tosses real meat to surreal
> dogs. No contest. The falls
> named "Devil's Throat" are papery
> white, a slowly folding envelope, sending
> a code word to God; something about
> live heroes dying in the jaws
> of murderous dogs. And at last, at least
> (dogs wreak, gods repair)
> an honored immaculate slowly folding shroud.

Evening. Department of Incidental Intelligence. We're flourishing here at the hotel for sixty dollars per day, while

Rolf, our young nature boy–Jesuit, is putting up nearby in Iguaçu for two dollars a night, including breakfast and laundry. Another item. Our windup party tomorrow night will gobble up more pesos than most Argentinians could earn in several years. One must confess to a deep shame.

I sense that Bob De Niro chooses his friends with extreme care, as most shy folk tend to do. But once made, a friend is a friend for good. Slow track, right destination, so to speak, whereas with others, the fast track seems to lead precisely nowhere.

I remember my qualms when "spiritual tactics" (means of helping the actors prepare for their part in the film as Jesuit priests) were first mentioned in New York. My sense at the time was that the sacred should not become a kind of tool or ploy or game, a chapter out of actors' school, ensuring a better act. This puts it crudely but perhaps accurately.

There may, on the other hand, be a better way to prepare such heroic parts as are demanded by the film; but if there is, I have yet to hear of it.

We have a lost soul in our midst playing a found one. Indeed most of us swing somewhere between lost and found, touching the one pole because we are death ridden and the other because God is good. But to play this game is to hover over a void and name it dry land (except of course in films, where anything credible is approved).

I'm found today. Yesterday I was quite at a loss. Thus goes life, a lost and found department.

*   *   *

Speaking of lost and found. A pair of demoiselles hovered about all week, somewhat woebegone groupies under the face paint. One of them confided, "We came from Buenos Aires because we heard Robert De Niro was here."

The soul of kindness itself, he invites them to dine with us more in the nature of a penance for the rest. In consequence, friendship creaks a bit, but of course prevails.

I wonder nonetheless at the emptiness of such workaday lives; the women undoubtedly pooled their worldly wages to come here, enchanted by a hero of the silver screen.

They also phoned Jeremy on arrival, seeking audience. But he pronounces the sirens boring and adroitly sidesteps their charms.

And now at length to the end of the adventure. Celebration prevailed last night; something known in the lingo as the "wrapup party." Some hundred and fifty of us gathered in a vast, utterly characterless ballroom; it reminded me of one of my nightmares—an inflated Kafkaesque prison cell.

In the course of the revelries, Paula, she of makeup skills, whispered hoarsely in my ear, "The worst Bar Mitzvah I've ever been condemned to attend!" At our table, Liam, Dan, Bob, son Raphael, and our friends, the three Onani Indians, made the complement. Liquids were in abundance, solids excruciatingly stone cold.

At the end, Roland's remarks were such as we've come to expect—precise and appropriate. He summoned the Indians for a bow and standing applause; they were as he said justly, "friends who made our film come to life."

Amen to that!

And alleluia too!